AMERICAN COMMUNICATION IN A GLOBAL SOCIETY

COMMUNICATION AND INFORMATION SCIENCE

A series of monographs,
treatises, and texts

Edited by
MELVIN J. VOIGT

University of California, San Diego

RHONDA J. CRANE • The Politics of International Standards: France and the Color TV War

GLEN FISHER • American Communication in a Global Society

VINCENT MOSCO • Broadcasting in the United States: Innovative Challenge and Organizational Control

KAARLE NORDENSTRENG AND HERBERT I. SCHILLER • National Sovereignty and International Communication: A Reader

In Preparation

JOHN J. GEYER • Reading as Information Processing

MICHEL GUITE • Telecommunications Policy: The Canadian Model

JOHN S. LAWRENCE AND BERNARD M. TIMBERG • Fair Use and Free Inquiry: Copyright Law and the New Media

ROBERT B. MEADOW • Politics as Communication

ITHIEL DE SOLA POOL • Retrospective Technology Assessment of the Telephone

CLAIRE K. SCHULTZ • Computer History and Information Access

AMERICAN COMMUNICATION IN A GLOBAL SOCIETY

Glen Fisher
Georgetown University

Ablex Publishing Corporation
Norwood, New Jersey 07648

Library of Congress Cataloging in Publication Data

Fisher, Glen H
  American communication in a global society.

  (Communication and information science)
  Bibliography: p.
  Includes index.
  1. United States—Relations (general) with foreign
countries.   2. Intercultural communication.   I. Title.
II. Series.
E840.2.F57   301.29'73   79-9331
ISBN   0-89391-025-2

ABLEX Publishing Corporation
355 Chestnut Street
Norwood, New Jersey 07648

CONTENTS

PREFACE

Both Americans and those who must deal with them have reason to consider the pattern and effect of American communication. To address oneself, however, to so large a subject as American communication in a global society is to ask for trouble even though the intention here is only to look to the agenda for approaching the subject rather than to engage in a comprehensive treatment of it. The ways in which the subject could be approached are so varied that it is important at the outset to note the background and resources for central ideas and data used here. Primarily, this book is an exercise in pulling together thinking from many sources and from many people professionally concerned with international communication processes, although the way that these ideas have been selected and brought together reflects my own vantage point. The reader should know what this vantage point is in order to understand why this particular direction has been chosen.

My attention was drawn to international communication questions most directly by a 1974–76 assignment to the State Department's Bureau of Educational and Cultural Affairs as Advisor for Policy Development. This was followed by a consultancy which has extended through the amalgamation of that Bureau, the United States Information Agency, and the Voice of America into the new International Communication Agency. In 1974 Assistant Secretary of State John Richardson, Jr. was engaged in a major initiative to encourage his own staff along with other leaders in the communication and educational and cultural exchange fields to think in some depth about changes taking place in the international communication environment and to recheck exchange activities for their consistency with new needs and priorities. Thus, life in the bureau was dominated by questions such as: why are we doing what we are doing? what should we be doing now and in the next few years? why? The reorganization then pending lent purpose to the search for an updated rationale. Many of the questions raised at that time have found their way into this book. Creation of the new Agency has added stimulation around Washington to continue the inquiry.

The analytical orientation most central in my approach to the international communication process has been a combination of sociology, anthropology, and social psychology. This reflects both my own academic background and my interest over a number of years in applying analytical conceptions from these fields to the psychological and cross-cultural dimension of foreign affairs.

My pattern of concerns is also that of a Foreign Service Officer, reflecting assignments in Latin America, the Philippines, the Department of State, briefly at the United Nations, and several times to the faculty of the Foreign Service Institute, where I could indulge my interest in area studies and psycho-cultural approaches to them. In overseas assignments I had frequent occasion to associate closely with my colleagues in the United States Information Service, sometimes because their activities were the most interesting in town, and sometimes because that was the normal course of embassy business.

There are, however, several more specific research ventures which have provided material for this study, and which explain my emphasis on the developing world and my choice of some of the illustrative material. During 1975–77, I was asked to undertake three pilot research projects to look for salient factors in current international communication relations that should be taken into account in planning Bureau of Educational and Cultural Affairs activities over the following two- to five-year period. The idea was that by starting with my social science conceptions of what to look for and a recognition of the issues as they had emerged in Bureau discussions, I could then explore the insight and judgment available from people working with exchange and communication activities abroad. This would enable me to produce the kind of "think piece" analysis that would sharpen the focus on trends and new factors which might affect the logic of a wide range of programs directed toward mutual understanding objectives.

The first of these studies took me to Indonesia, Malaysia, Singapore, and the Philippines. After digesting the results of that work back in the Bureau, a second study was undertaken in sample countries in the Middle East and Africa: Egypt, Iran, Kenya, Zambia, and Cameroon. (This was before the Iranian revolution that forced the departure of the Shah.) A third study concerned communication and exchange relationships with India. This U.S.-based project depended on specialists in India-related activities in Washington and in several university area study centers. In all, these projects involved more than 200 systematic discussions with professional-level observers and communicators in nine countries and in the United States.

The overseas research method, if it could be called that, was simply to pick the minds of selected officers in U.S. diplomatic posts, of resident nonofficial Americans, of local citizens and officials, and of third country specialists—people chosen for their pertinent experience on the scene and for their professional basis for judgment. This sample represented, of course, a wide range of people: cultural affairs officers in embassies, deans of local universities, American businessmen and missionaries, Peace Corps representatives, former Fulbright scholars, communication research specialists, local government officials, and so forth.

Sections of Chapter 4 that relate to the international flow of news were first inspired by my participation in a project initiated by Professor Philip Horton of the Fletcher School of Law and Diplomacy. The purpose of the project was to bring together journalists and news managers from the First and Third Worlds in a New York Conference to consider their differing perspectives on today's largely one-way flow of news and information. The planning, the conference itself, and a subsequent research project that studied the conference's effects provided a concentrated exposure. Later conferences and discussions have added more, of course.

While the analysis and the conclusions drawn are my own, and no statement of official policy is implied, the ideas of many people in and out of government have been a rich resource. The encouragement of a number of people has also been important. Along with the Bureau of Educational and Cultural Affairs, this direction of inquiry has found support in two academic institutions. The Georgetown University School of Foreign Service, with which I am now associated, has been actively looking to these new directions in foreign affairs analysis. The Edward R. Murrow Center for Public Diplomacy at the Fletcher School of Law and Diplomacy has also been a source of ideas and encouragement, starting with the year I spent there in 1970–71 on an earlier research project.

1

AN INTERNATIONAL SYSTEM DEMANDS QUALITY COMMUNICATION

It is difficult to overestimate the importance of the role that communication will play in an ever more crowded and interconnected world. How the United States manages its predominant share will affect not only the well-being of Americans, but that of much of the rest of the world as well. The key question for the remainder of this century, then, is what the function of American communication will be in a world which by its all-encompassing communication technology now has enough of a central nervous system to become, de facto, a global society—a society which by its interdependence already has to interact and resolve problems on a global scale.

The United States is the world's most communicating nation. It is the largest producer, consumer, and exporter of information of all kinds, and the innovating genius in equipment and information management as well. The U.S. is the most advanced "information society" and, as such, has long made the greatest impact abroad by its influence on media everywhere and by the messages it transmits that penetrate other cultures and affect changing ways of life in the modern era. Its political and economic messages—intended and otherwise—have dominated international relations debate for decades, especially since World War II.

The American role in all this is changing, and probably will change even more. The possibilities of space-age technology will transform the international communication network in ways that we can now only imagine. But political, social, and psychological factors may be more important than the equipment. At the least, as more national leaders become conscious of the importance of international communication and information systems to their societies, the more the debate will intensify as to how those systems are to be used, and what substance is to be communicated. Of course, the total communication system goes much beyond the central flow by electronic channels. Travel, the press, books and literature, education, international conferences, business negotiation, artistic expression, commercial exchange, technical assistance, and much more add to the communication flow of more obvious radio, television, and satellite transmission.

It follows that the way in which peoples and nations communicate in such an unfolding information-centered and message-dependent world deserves close attention as an integral part of the international relations process. The consequences of misperception and unreliable information are too central to the management of international business at all levels to leave communication factors off the international relations agenda. Along with the policy-maker and those who actually do the international interacting, the concerned citizen too will need to engage his thinking on this dimension just to be internationally literate.

What is now a high priority task, one to which the pages that follow are dedicated, is to make an assessment of the current state of world communication relations, particularly of the trends and factors which most need to be taken into account. In large part, this is a matter of assessing the state of American communication within international society.

As this is being written the U.S. Government has just launched a new International Communication Agency, merging the previous United States Information Agency, the Department of State's Bureau of Educational and Cultural Affairs, and the Voice of America into a new entity. This new agency will take a new grip on the official side of America's communication efforts abroad. In dropping the term "information," official planners see the era for propaganda as having passed. The new emphasis will be on two-way bridges which will enhance the understanding process on all sides.

Realistically, of course, what the U.S. government does or does not do in its official programs is a relatively minor aspect of the total spectrum of world communication. But its deliberations serve as a focal point for looking at the changes that have taken place in the arena in which the United States would communicate, and the time frame suggested by the government's policy problem can serve a broader inquiry as well: The agencies now being repackaged were post-World War II creations; their age since conception is about 25 years. The question, then, is what basically has occurred in these years to prompt a new conceptualization and incarnation? Most especially, what has happened in recent years to highlight the need to trade in the old model for a newer one?

THE CHANGES ARE REAL
AND FUNDAMENTAL

The main factors which have so changed the international communication environment are probably well known to the reader; listing them will hardly break new ground. But it is useful to review them, for it is in their combination that the full significance of the changes in the post-war era emerge.

First, in the last 25 years or so, the number of people in the world has doubled, the number of their independent countries has more than doubled, and the number of literate human beings has grown dramatically. This is a profound change in the communication environment even if there were no others. To paraphrase the title of George Ball's book *Diplomacy for a Crowded World (1976),* what we are talking about is *communication* for a crowded world.

As more nations have emerged on the world scene, the proportion with nonWestern cultures, and with all the "nonconventional" wisdom that this implies, has risen. The amount of international communication that is significantly cross-cultural has correspondingly increased. Different ideas and thought patterns which have, for example, posed problems for Americans and Japanese in such fields as corporation decision-making or democratic processes are now joined by new variations in culturally-influenced outlooks from Tanzania, Bangladesh, or the People's Republic of China. Issues range from the meaning of law and economic institutions to human rights and the proper role of the press. Americans have difficulties enough talking on the same wavelength with Western world countries which share common roots, and with whom they have considerable practice. Impediments are compounded in cases where there is little experience in sustained dialogue except at the most elite and cosmopolitan level.

While impossible to quantify, the number of people who now effectively participate in a modernized world and compete for access to knowledge and information along with other resources necessary to a modern standard of living has enlarged to critical mass proportions. There *has* been a lot of economic and social development in the last quarter century. This is seen in the expansion of middle classes in terms of standards of occupation and income; it is seen even more clearly in terms of aspiration to, or identification with, these standards. In glancing over UNESCO statistics (1976), one notes that between 1965 and 1975 the number of students in higher education in countries around the world typically doubled. One might claim that for purposes of communication analysis, India, for example, is a nation of 200 million people identifying with middle sector concerns—a facet of India often overlooked in the Western image of that country. Or, it can be argued, the overall social structure of the world has changed dramatically since the end of the World War II, producing all the stresses and strains we hear so much about. One of the psychosocial and psychopolitical impacts on the world communication process is the demand for a new international economic order.

We see, then, that the technological means of communication have expanded far faster than the ability to digest the consequences. Sometimes the problems are of modest proportions. As television became standard entertainment in urban centers around the world, the international community in Kuala Lumpur came to recognize which evenings were inauspicious for inviting their Malaysian friends to social functions—those when "Hawaii Five-O" was on the tube. Other problems are more far-reaching. Now that Indonesia has gone to satellite-assisted television to reach its further island population, someone has to decide what to program. Can TV help to ease the transition of cultural values from the traditional to those which support participation in modern life? Can it do this without creating psychological and social chaos?

Transistorized radio reception has now reached the all-encompassing proliferation foreseen when its possibilities became apparent in the immediate post-war years. While it has become a nuisance in the developed countries for those who seek peace and quiet in public buses or on the beaches, its ubiquity in country markets from Afghanistan to Zambia has multiplied enormously the number of people who participate in the international communication network. Third world governments consider radio their primary means of relaying their messages to their populations; it is a national resource for communicating development information, for pushing national integration, and often for controlling the political process. The first step in many a coup d'etat is to take over the national radio network. Now television provides the potential for adding revolutionary sight to sound.

As press services and their products reach even further and faster, there is growing disquiet regarding their control and management from the West. The talk is of a "new international information order" to give developing countries greater participation in what is seen as a resource to which access is as important as to international food resources and manufactured goods. Computerized technology and its applications have expanded with little regard for national boundaries; data banks, medical diagnosis resource centers, scientific analysis programming, insurance calculations, are planned with multinational use in mind. Computer-assisted educational techniques are beginning to go international.

It is even reported that when a Scandinavian city fire department decided to install an information retrieval system to give instant readouts of essential fire fighting information for any given address, an American company presented the most attractive bid. Now in place, it works, right down to spelling out the fastest route to the fire—all from Cleveland. The distance simply does not make much difference.

THE INCREASINGLY IMPORTANT
INTERDEPENDENCE FACTOR

Perhaps the most important consideration for looking to the quality of international communication is the matter of coping with interdependence. This is not a new circumstance for mankind, nor a new subject for the reader. But it is increasingly significant, both in the degree that it affects everyone's life and in the greater recognition it currently receives in decision-making and problem solving. The idea of *dependence* has long been established in much of the world where all kinds of domestic issues have hinged upon what happened in more powerful neighbor nations—in the part of the dog that wagged the tail. American travellers abroad have often heard local people comment that American presidential elections are more important to them then their own. But now it is also becoming obvious to Americans that what used to be their *domestic* problems are now *international* ones; where they used to be largely in command of their own public policy decisions, they now have to seek solutions on the multilateral or even global level. The distinction between domestic and international is more blurred every year. The Americans' options are not all their own. The energy crunch has made it real. Perhaps the view of the earth from the moon helped provide a philosophical appreciation for the relative insignificance of separate national problems in a "global village."

So our American lifestyle is not, and will not be, all of our own making. Beyond energy, much of our total economy is basically international. A large proportion of our big corporations are multinational in concept and, to an advanced degree, in operation. More than 20% of all United States international trade is said to consist of the internal transactions of multinational corporations (Aspen Institute for Humanistic Studies, 1975). The environment itself cannot be managed on a country-by-country basis—there is pollution in the oceans, carbon monoxide in the atmosphere, and interference in the use of crowded radio frequencies in the air waves. Even though the United States controls its own population increase, it feels the pressure from elsewhere as it tries to decide what to do about six million illegal immigrants with all their needs for jobs, education, social services, and their problems of exploitation occasioned by their uncertain status. American wheat prices depend on the size of the Russian crop. The U.S. policy on exporting soy beans must take into account the needs of those who depend on U.S. production—Japan, for example. Even America's ocean shipping links with the rest of the world depend on the maritime laws and regulations of Panama and Liberia!

An overly sanguine acceptance of interdependence is unrealistic. While it may appear that the new internationalism the interdependent circumstances seems to imply would come to supersede the nationalistic conflict of the past, the fact is that all this interconnectedness is a *conflict-producing condition*. There is more opportunity for conflicting interests to come to the surface, more occasion for abrasion, especially as more private groups have to conduct some degree of international relations in their spheres of specialization. All this places an enormous demand on our collective ability to communicate effectively. It places pressure on an ever larger number of people—at least on the "elites," in political science terms—to be able to bridge gaps of differing society, culture and national experience to negotiate their international business.

THE "GLOBAL SOCIETY" APPROACH

Most probably, using a term like "global society" will put the reader off a bit. "Global" is a fuzzy conception; it is too grandiosely abstract for most intellectual tastes. And "global society" seems like an idealistic or utopian projection that goes too far beyond the reality of the here and now. But its use is intended to serve the analytical purpose of helping to explain precisely what *is* going on in the here and now. The term suggests analysis without regard for political boundaries. From a sociological point of view, we already interact on global societal dimensions, and it is useful to pursue the functions of international communication in these terms. Whether a society is big or small, communication is essential to making the parts fit together and to accomplishing tasks that require coordinated behavior. For many analytical purposes, global society is not, of course, an appropriate level of approach. In fact, for some purposes, even American society is too broad a canvas. But if we are to consider the structure and function of *international* communication, we need to address ourselves to the social reality that this implies. Therefore, we look to the inner workings of a "global society."[1]

How far have we gone along the global scale? Certainly not all inhabitants of the globe identify with so immense a mass. But the social–psychological underpinnings for a "society" are advancing as more members of more world communities are feeling their interaction with a world-sized collectivity of human beings. There is no world government, and perhaps never will be, but a number of aspects of a global governmental function are now embodied in international organizations and in conceptions of international law. There are relatively few world-wide institutions, but there are some that nearly fit the definition: the Catholic Church, Associated Press, Sony, Rotary International, the postal service, the United Nations Food and Agriculture Organization, and the International Olympics.

"Society" implies existence of a common culture—shared knowledge and beliefs, patterns of association and custom. On this "globe" one is actually impressed with the diversity and contrast even among peoples of the traditional Western world. Yet an advanced degree of internationalized common culture does extend around the world even though most people only observe bits and pieces of it. Technology, commerce, and finance provide a common base. Western dress, literature, and music are found in most urban areas. Travelers' accommodations are fairly standardized. English is rapidly becoming the world's lingua franca. Thus, many people in many nations participate in an internationalized common culture at least part of the time, or with part of their psyches.

Therefore, the thesis here is that the time is not too early, nor the approach too abstract, to think in terms of a global society for analytical purposes, and to look to the role that communication will play in providing the central nervous system that will allow a society approaching perhaps three billion people to function with some minimum amount of cooperation and coordination. Population density, competition for limited resources, even the relatively recently acquired potential for mankind's self-destruction suggest it is necessary to venture onto this level of sociological assessment. Even if concern is essentially confined to one's own national or ethnic group, there is a need to be aware of the way in which the inescapable social forces of a global society impinge on one's own social unit.

[1]As one attempt to place this approach in the context of international relations theory, see Evan Luard, *Types of International Society* (New York: Free Press, 1976).

COMMUNICATION AND
PUBLIC DIPLOMACY

More communication about more issues produces a different kind of international relations process than the conception held of it in traditional diplomacy and still presented in many university courses on international affairs. Certainly public psychological factors now assume ever more importance in foreign affairs decision-making and negotiation. We are in an era of public diplomacy in that government actions must be increasingly responsive to the views and judgments of their peoples, particularly as media services make their impact and as public groups articulate their concerns more effectively. Even the most authoritarian governments can no longer ignore their better educated, informed, and urbanized constituencies. Hence, how publics get their information and how they are predisposed to react to it becomes as important a consideration in foreign affairs as real-politik strategy or the private views of national leaders, whether or not these publics are objective or "rational" in their perceptions.[2]

The public diplomacy dimension becomes even more significant as a stream of nongovernmental transnational linkages and activities also becomes part of the international relations process. Transnational corporations were mentioned above. Labor groups, religious and educational institutions, nonprofit organizations and service clubs, scientists, political parties, book publishers, and newsmen carry their share of negotiating and decision-making responsibilities.

First attention in the public diplomacy realm usually is directed toward the officially sponsored public communication of governments. As we noted above, for Americans this is now the International Communication Agency, its mission being considered anew as it is projected ahead. Agents of any official information program today find that their efforts are but a small part of an ever-growing communication flow that goes on anyway to create images, report events, and suggest their meaning. It is easy to overestimate the capacity of purposeful information or exchange programs to change the terms of dialogue, or to influence patterns of thinking. When the United States undertook its post-war information activities, the objective was to balance out the often distorted presentation of American life that was otherwise presented by the mass media, hostile propaganda, or by accumulations of misinformation. Today the total outflow of information coming just from within the United States is so complex and so much greater than it was 25 years ago that such an objective is hardly credible. Planned official efforts are

[2]This idea is developed in more detail in Glen H. Fisher, *Public Diplomacy and the Behavioral Sciences* (Bloomington: Indiana University Press, 1972).

dwarfed by the magnitude and volume of the uncoordinated commercial aɪ.d private channels of mass communication.

In a former era we also conceived our international information and educational activities to be an effort to jump over the heads of the officials, governments, and leaders of other societies and speak directly to "the masses." This is a kind of thinking that time has passed by. Even third world societies have passed beyond that point of manipulation. Their own elites are well in charge. In any case, the content of the larger mass flow from the United States itself is not subject to governmental monitoring. Americans insist on freedom in the flow of information. Controlling the output is an option that the United States Government, unlike many others, does not have. The problem for a purposeful U.S. governmental program is to define its unique function as a government program—what can it communicate that is not already communicated? What are the essential gaps? How can it facilitate a constructive flow?

In looking back on American communicative activities of the last two decades, it is obvious that Cold War assumptions had much to do with the style and content of both governmental and private programs. Radio Liberty, Radio Free Europe, and the Voice of America reflected Cold War concerns. Ideological competition dominated the scene; judgments were polarized—if you were not for democracy and the United States, you were the enemy. Neutralism was simply sinful, an outlook noted with some flair by Townsend Hoopes in his *The Devil and John Foster Dulles* (1974). This outlook was evident in Latin American policy, for example. Any perception of a Marxist hue in a political movement went a long way to preprogram our often simplistically negative views of that movement. John Stoessinger in his *Nations in Darkness* (1971) and Louis Halle in his *The Cold War as History* (1967) document the way that Cold War perceptions, and often misperceptions, became the frame of reference for policy decisions on all sides of the "cold" conflict. USIS activities abroad, international visitor programs, and even the Fulbright academic exchange were seen first as assets in winning the Cold War. Private businesses judged investment climates in these terms, and citizens travelling abroad saw themselves as ambassadors and spokesmen for the free enterprise and democratic side of the ideological confrontation.

So today's communication priorities are changing as we recognize, perhaps belatedly, that the Cold War is over, at least as pursued in the 1950s and 60s. Today we live with much more acceptance of pluralism, more respect for differences, with less sense of bipolar ideological division. It is a time when naive propaganda or ethnocentric self-advertising seem anachronistic as well as ineffective.

Actually, as will be discussed at greater length in a subsequent chapter, the substance of the international dialogue also has changed in emphasis. The essence of the change is from political–ideological matters to economic or economic–ideological. Interdependence is a large part of the reason. There is so much more now to be managed in the economic sphere. Part of the explanation is events. The Viet Nam experience along with the introspection occasioned by Watergate and related domestic matters, have led Americans to pause in their tendency to be prescriptive regarding political institutions and practices abroad. On the other side, especially in developing countries where people are already frustrated with trying to make American models work, the troubling view of American involvement in Viet Nam served as a catalyst to make leaders reconsider. They found that American political models may not be so transferrable, and not necessarily very satisfying in a different cultural milieu. Such leaders came to identify less closely with the American experience. It is not, and will not be their experience. More of this will be discussed in Chapter 3.

In sum, looking ahead we see that a lot of strain is going to be placed on the international communication process and on American leadership in it. We have often judged the quality of communication in terms of the good will that is generated between the United States and other nations. That goal is laudable enough, but probably superficial. In an era of interdependence, with real problems facing mankind for survival, *accurate* understanding is of higher priority. Recent studies of decision-making indicate that national choices are too often a function of an unacceptable degree of misperception on all sides—sometimes misperceptions by leaders, sometimes by their publics, usually by both. Within a country, decision makers and their constituents often reinforce each other's inaccurate interpretation of events. People are the prisoners of images.[3]

Unfortunately, we know relatively little about the international communication process itself. To the extent that we have thought about it at all, we usually have approached it in an unstudied manner, a sure formula for perpetuating ethnocentric views of how it works, and dangerous misperceptions of the U.S. position in it. Following chapters will attempt to isolate significant elements and hold them up for examination. If the effort is successful, some contribution may have been made in setting the agenda for attending to the communication dimension.

[3]Again, see Stoessinger, and also Irving L. Janis, *Victims of Groupthink* (New York: Houghton Mifflin, 1972).

2
ASSETS AND LIABILITIES GOING INTO THE 1980s

The United States has celebrated its 200th birthday, ventured into space, called it a day in Viet Nam, and has become more aware than ever that its future well-being depends on the way that things go internationally. For all the domestic strains of Watergate and the need to adjust posture after a less-than-satisfying withdrawal from Southeast Asia, the U.S. remains the international center of gravity—economically, militarily, technologically, and probably intellectually. The question to consider here is where this leaves the United States in the conduct of its international communication relationships. This may not be the usual way of looking at the state of a nation's foreign affairs, but it is a logical way given the ever more important part that communication plays in the total process.

The tricky task is to gain an objective perspective. How can one place oneself emotionally and intellectually outside the entire international communication system to make impartial judgments? It is improbable that an American writer can, and equally improbable that American readers would be able to join him in objectivity if he did succeed. But a degree of detachment is worth a try, and that is the goal that will be pursued here. Imagine, perhaps, the view from Malta, Switzerland, Costa Rica, Hong Kong, or similar places where people do not have the same vested interest in the United States' central position that Americans have, but do not have a motive for being blindly critical either. We are looking, within reasonable limits, for the gift to "see ourselves as others see us" as Robert Burns suggested quite a long time ago. First we will look at some of the factors which give Americans broad options for exercising leadership, then at some of the communication liabilities.

The initial factor to consider is the sheer volume of communication traffic which flows to and from the United States. It might be useful here to try to picture the centrality of the U.S. in world communication flows. For example, geographers have a graphic device for showing this kind of thing for transportation routes in a given area. First they sketch in the routes on a map—let us say inter-island shipping in the Philippines (this is the application where I first saw the approach used). Then they make the lines darker and broader depending on the volume of products that travel each route, so that the lines become thick and prominent as they converge on the most important traffic centers, looking something like drawings of the human blood vessel system in a physiology textbook. The big arteries and veins come together at the heart, the large ones go to the lungs, head, and major muscles, lesser ones go to the extremities. For the Philippines, such a map shows immediately how important Manila and Cebu City (in the Central Visayas) are in the total inter-island shipping system. If the same were done for international communication, the lines carrying the heavy volume of messages would converge on the United States. It would be hard to imagine the system working at all if the United States were removed from the network.

COMMUNICATING IN A TECHNOLOGICAL AGE—IN ENGLISH

What gives the United States so central a position? Americans themselves would cite their highly advanced communications technological capacity, the advantage of a free society, and their own international initiatives in business, travel and commerce. In short, Americans simply have more to say and more occasion to say it. But from a more detached view, the emphasis might be placed somewhat differently: *The United States is the world's prime reservoir of technology and its uses available via the English language.* This goes a long way to explain those heavy lines radiating from the United States on the communication traffic map. Certainly the advantage of being at the center of technology is clear in a world which runs on technology and one where technological application and economic development go hand-in-hand. But when one adds that today English has become *the basic international language* for technology, commerce, finance, science, and travel, the favorable position of the United States is still clearer.

The role that English has come to play in the world today deserves particular attention. Its use is spreading at a dramatic rate; the implications of this have been little studied. It long has had wide and strategic use, of course, as the language of the British, American, Canadian, and Australian peoples. If anyone had anything important to say in any part of the far-flung British Empire, he was expected to say it in English. The long arm of American and British literature and entertainment has been recognized for many generations. But as one travels it is apparent that English is no longer simply the common language spoken by the British, the Americans, their cousins and colonial protégés. It is the *international* language of science and technology, *the language of access to modern life.* The trend is well advanced. The world is on the verge of a lingua franca, and this fact is a highly significant aspect of today's communication revolution. This culture-bridging facility joins developments in literacy, electronic media, satellites, and television in its potential and impact.

Finding that one needs to use English is becoming a more neutral matter politically. There seems to be less complaint that it is an affront to one's national identity, or that its use is a cultural or ideological sellout to the hegemony of the West despite the symbolic importance of national languages. While Americans might still be well-advised to be discreet in their proprietary satisfaction with the trend, there is little need to be apologetic in aiding the English learning process. The world may be, in fact, over the hump of psychological reluctance to letting one language serve an international role. The objective sought by one-world idealists might be nearer than we realize. Actually, the ability to speak the same language does not guarantee cooperation and agreement—it might make disagreement clearer—but the potential contribution of a common language to mutual understanding can hardly be overestimated.

Examples of the trend abound. In much of the developing world it is assumed that to participate in modernity and its benefits, English is essential. It is the key to upward mobility, the way to be plugged into the mainstream of specialized knowledge, the symbol of prestige in many elite circles. For example, in Iran the chancellor of a leading university, himself a Francophile, discussed aspirations for language use in instruction. While in ten years he hoped that undergraduate courses would all be in Farsi for maximum diffusion of knowledge, graduate instruction would be in English. In the People's Republic of China, English is now the principal foreign language taught in the school system.

Historically, French probably came nearest to being the international language, at least in such areas as diplomacy, literature, and the arts. It is still widely used, but is losing its grip in competition with English. In France itself, it has been reported that there is a growing tendency for French scientists to publish their work first in English—regretfully but realistically. Being linguistically patriotic to French does not get them far in international scientific circles. All these inroads being made by English produces bitter debate in France, as those acquainted with the French emotional attachment to French culture can appreciate.

In Cameroon, where French and British colonies were joined, both English and French were made official languages. None of the 200 local languages used in the area was considered, for achieving national unity was already difficult enough. Actually, French is much more widely spoken than English, and could become the single common national language. But even French-speaking educational leaders argue for continued emphasis on English for the access it gives to the modern world. They do not want to see English phased out simply in the interest of moving to a more practical one-language educational base.

English is easily becoming the second language choice for national groups whose own language is not Western to begin with, or has not competed for international usage. In Scandanavia, Belgium, Denmark, and even Germany, becoming bilingual in English is simply part of a decent education—a circumstance which makes life easier for American tourists. One, incidentally, recently reported overhearing an argument on a European train (between a Swede and a Dane) as to which of their languages had best retained its purity. They argued in English. It has been suggested that in international meetings Italians have less influence than they might otherwise have because too few leading Italian political leaders speak English. I noticed while browsing in bookshops in both Egypt and Iran that a wide variety of Russian-produced books were available in paperback and at popular prices. Subjects ranged over common technical areas and into some politically-related fields; they were intended for volume sales in these Farsi and Arabic-speaking countries. The language used in the books? English, of course.

In exchanges made in speeches between Egyptian President Sadat and Israeli Prime Minister Begin before their historic 1977 meeting in Jerusalem, the language directed to the other side was English. President Sadat spoke through no interpreter to send his message—it was English. Prime Minister Begin interrupted a speech in Hebrew to state in English his willingness to have Sadat visit. Even at the meeting, during the formal Hebrew and Arabic speeches in the Israeli Knesset, when Begin wanted to make an extemporaneous aside for Sadat's benefit, he switched to English.

Another indicator of the trend is seen in the preferences of those who go abroad for education or technical training. Even those favorably predisposed ideologically are reluctant to go to the Soviet Union and invest in learning Russian. It is a lost investment thereafter. France is also a second choice for the same reason except for those in Francophone countries. Japan is out of the question. And if you want to be an airline pilot on the international routes, you must learn English along with navigation if you expect to speak to control towers around the world. As computer data banks become still more interlaced internationally, English will have further occasion to become entrenched.

The full significance of the English language revolution, however, is yet to be seen. It will depend on the degree to which the life styles and patterns of thinking which go with English become part of a growing internationalized common culture.

TRENDS TOWARD AN INTERNATIONAL
CULTURE—AND THE U.S. ROLE IN IT

International communication through modern history has been made easier by the general similarity in the cultures of Western nations, and by the influence of that homogenized mainstream outside the West. Issues were defined according to Western conventions, the basic decisions of international relations were made, and standards for "rational" behavior and thinking were set. While nonWestern cultures existed in great number and variety, the people of these societies had to do the adapting in their international activities. The Western world made little effort to go half way. They either suffered the strange and provincial world views which prevailed outside Christendom, or tried to bring enlightenment—which meant Westernization.

Since World War II, two counter-trends have significantly changed this communication environment. On the one hand, the nations with nonWestern culture and tradition have become more prominent actors on the international stage, and the real diversity and multicultural character of the world's peoples has been forced on world attention. This alters the nature of international dialogue and negotiating. From the 51 countries which signed the United Nations Charter in 1945, the number of flags now displayed before the U.N. headquarters on New York's First Avenue has passed 150. NonWestern blocs form and change, depending on the issues, to wield considerable power. Much of the international debate now goes into stroking national identity and discussing issues which are of special interest to the nonWestern countries. Conceptions like a "new international economic order" dominate proceedings; when Western countries negotiate for access to nonWestern energy resources, they face this new view of economic purpose. New approaches to law and social justice, and new tactics considered appropriate for achieving leverage—terrorism, for example—become very real and have to be dealt with.

Now Western powers find that *they* need to do some of the adapting in their patterns of thinking when they are involved in nonWestern situations. Assumptions about the use of military force as an instrument of national policy have been shaken as Western powers have tried to use it in very nonWestern areas. For the United States, military involvement in Korea and then in Viet Nam was its first modern large-scale experience in warfare outside a Western context since the war with Japan, and that was fought largely in traditional ways. All the assumptions about military leadership, public mobilization, the logic of public opinion, and even what constituted "unsupportable" losses had to be relearned. When the factors that really determined performance and outcome could not be handled in Western statistical analysis formulas, judgments became unreliable and the U.S. found it difficult to program its overwhelming military power against predictable results. Confronting guerrilla warfare at the village level was particularly difficult, as the gulfs between cultures and patterns of thinking were so directly related to the course of events at that level.

Thus, by one set of trends, attention is called to the multicultural reality of the world, and the effects that this has on today's international communication processes. However, by another set of trends, this diversity is being blurred by increasing acceptance of the customs and life styles of what might be considered an international culture. This helps bridge the differences for those who must interact internationally, but it is a pervading influence on the life styles of the less internationally-minded as well. For the most part, this internationalized culture is a composite of Western conventions, and increasingly, a reflection of contemporary America. This trend reinforces the American position in the middle of the international communication system.

The evidence is clear enough. One can travel from almost any one of the world's large cities to another and get along with only minor adjustments while conducting business with that part of the local population that shares international culture or provides the facilities for it. The international mainstream is seen in fashions on the street, hotels, airlines offices, advertising, automobile agencies, newsstands, and radios blaring popular music. Modern cities need fast food services, and the most efficient are the familiar international chains: McDonald's in Tokyo and Paris, Wimpy's in London and Cairo. Only a block from where I used to live on a quiet street in the Altamira section of Caracas, one now cannot miss the ubiquitous Kentucky Fried Chicken. Not all of this is of U.S. origin. Chinese restaurants and Bata shoes cover the globe; sauna baths and sukiyaki houses are not far behind. And from whatever the source, plastic housewares and toys are making the country markets of Java and Guatemala look much less "typical" to the visitor today.

More important is that part of international culture which is less visible, the customs of the mind. Especially as one defines modern culture as knowledge in such fields as marketing, science and technology, finance, industrial techniques, or arts and entertainment, internationalization of habits of thinking has gone a long way. At least in certain contexts, there is some global homogeneity in ideas and assumptions. Possibly it is more accurate to say that there has been a vast increase in the number of people who can live simultaneously in two cultural contexts—that of their own local society, and the international. As more transnational groups come into existence—international civil servants, athletes, entertainers, professional societies, and multinational corporations—more people will have occasion to be international in one part of their mind.

In the early 1960s John Useem noted that people engaged in the technical assistance and economic development field were generating their own international subculture (Useem et al., 1963). He called them "men in the middle of the third culture" as for purposes of designing, negotiating, and carrying out cooperative projects, the specialists in both extending and receiving assistance had to step outside their own cultures to participate in what has become a new language and set of customs associated with managing assistance projects. Today, one might say that this "third culture" reality has expanded to include the brokers in many fields of international cooperation. And again the American role has become salient.

In some situations this international culture supplies a satisfying identity-defining function that goes well beyond the practicalities of international communication itself. It becomes the basic culture for many people. In some developing countries a substantial part of the new urban middle sectors are frustrated because their own national culture has not changed fast enough to meet their own psychological needs. Their traditional society did not provide for modern middle classes or new industrialists or professional elites, and it does not now provide a sense of identity or give satisfaction or status. Even that which is seen from the outside as the finest in traditional cultural expression, for example, Balinese dancing or Egyptian archaelogical wonders, is still seen as backward or without prestige in establishing oneself in competition with a modern world. These new groups would rather be renowned for accomplishment in the modern world on its own terms. To them, the international culture is the good life, and they want to identify with it and practice it. These people are not nationalistically trying to prevent the inroads of foreign things; they are the opposite of xenophobic. The more, the better; access to communication with the United States and Europe is essential. In sociological terms, their "reference group" includes foreign and modern people whom they would emulate. They want to be informed by international news services, be entertained by American movies, watch American television in English even if it is a bit hard to understand. They want to receive *Time* and *Newsweek, Paris Match,* the *London Economist,* or the *Far Eastern Economic Review.* They want to be up to date on fashions and music, and live in modern styles. In effect, they are in conflict with their own mainstream culture, and are opting for the international. It is their solution to a cultural identity problem.

For the larger part of such societies, however, the onslaught of international culture is a serious threat to the cultural values which have provided integration and meaning to daily life. In these cases the heavy one-way flow from the outside poses severe public policy problems for leaders and planners. This will be discussed further in Chapter 4.

Still, whether welcomed or not, the United States is the principal source for international culture. Few other societies compete seriously, and if they do, the variation from American standards and practices is not great. Few now turn to the Soviet Union for access to the international culture and its advantages; it is simply not a credible competitor. Actually, the contrast between the Soviet and Western models in this regard seems to be increasing, a trend of some importance in international communication even though the ledger is not kept as it was in Cold War days.

COLLEGE PROFESSOR TO THE WORLD

A third factor which places the United States in the forefront of international communication is the role that it plays, directly or indirectly, as college professor to the world. This is especially evident as one considers the combination of American educational resources: technological education in English, with laboratories, a mass student body, and high development of teaching materials and techniques for delivering education to the student. Whatever the shortcomings of the American higher education system as seen domestically, from the vantage point abroad where tradition-bound, procedure-encrusted systems are only beginning to change, or where resources are limited, the U.S. educational smorgasbord looks inviting indeed. As diplomatic relations were finally established with the People's Republic of China, their senior scholars began to arrive on American university campuses even before the new ambassadors had assumed their posts. Some 500–700 were expected the first year; perhaps 10,000 in several years.

Part of the educational traffic is shared with other English-speaking technological centers of course—England, Canada, and Australia, for example. For the former French colonial countries, France is the educational magnet. But the trend is with English, and with applied knowledge and how-to-do-it approaches even in the social sciences. Computerized information storing and processing itself is a culmination of this.

The significance for enhancing an American capacity to communicate with the world is that as the U.S. becomes the educational center in so many fields, and as its foreign graduates multiply and even undertake professional leadership or teaching in their own countries, the common foundation of knowledge, interests, and experience that facilitates effective dialogue with America expands. Not only is this important for the academic fields concerned, but when a degree of mutual comprehension and habits of cooperation are built into the relations among influential elites, the likelihood of intergovernmental cooperation is also enhanced. The existence of a certain critical mass of informed people who collaborate internationally as a matter of habit and routine helps ease potentially dangerous international disputes as these groups recognize larger common purposes, and are influential in reducing misperceptions and in rationalizing conflicts of interest that arise outside their own fields. They tend to supply something of a gyroscope effect in maintaining a sense of direction and stability in international relationships. This has even been true in the case of relations with adversaries, as seen in the result of intellectual and academic exchange with communist-ruled states.

There are now about 250,000 foreign students in the United States, with large contigents from Taiwan, Iran, India, Nigeria, and Venezuela contributing substantially to the total. The numbers increased strongly in the 1960s, a decade in which the total number of students enrolled in institutions of higher learning outside their own countries more than doubled, from 239,000 to 529,000. About one-third came to the United States.[1] In the 1970s, the numbers coming to the United States increased even more sharply for students from petroleum-producing countries.

This has not all happened spontaneously. The process has been greatly assisted by institutions dedicated to facilitating exchange, such as the Institute of International Education, the American Friends of the Middle East, or Operation Crossroads for Africa. Private programs such as those of the Rockefeller and Ford Foundations in the 1950s and 60s were singularly important, as were the fellowships extended by many American colleges and universities. Exchanges at the pre-college level were promoted by the American Field Service, the Experiment in International Living, Youth for Understanding, and a number of other programs.

But it was government-sponsored programs that combined volume

[1]From *UNESCO Statistical Yearbook* (1973, p. 115).

and selectivity. Foremost of these programs was the series of legislative enactments generally known as the Fulbright Program. Conceived with little realization of the force that it was to become, it began in 1946 simply as an amendment to a Surplus Property Act when Congress was looking for ways to spend U.S. funds generated in foreign countries that could not practically be converted into U.S. currency. It was the inspiration of Senator J. William Fulbright, himself a former Rhodes Scholar and university president. Fulbright saw it as a program to build intellectual bridges to countries that had just demonstrated the need for it in World War II, and thereby foster a deeper mutual understanding. Since that time the Fulbright Program has sponsored more than 42,000 Americans pursuing studies in 110 foreign countries, and more than 78,000 foreign scholars in the United States. In the process, it has helped establish linkages with international colleagues, and has provided that all too limited resource—first hand experience with the reality of other places and problems. Over the years it spawned a system of commissions and committees at home and abroad to select participants, and in general to promote international educational cooperation. It is often cited as an outstanding example of what can be accomplished through the cooperation of government and private institutions in pursuing objectives beyond the capacities of either. Its success is evident by the extent to which it has been imitated, and in the list of international leaders among the alumni, as well as by the contribution it has made to the development of academic fields on an international basis. In fact, the program boasts of having provided exchange experience in the earlier careers of 14 presidents or chancellors, 23 prime ministers or premiers, and 251 cabinet members in 75 countries (United States Department of State, Bureau of Educational and Cultural Affairs, 1976).

This stream of exchange visitors has been substantially augmented by training in the United States related to development activities around the world, and also by the use of American professionals in a wide range of overseas technical assistance programs that often were essentially educational ventures, sometimes directly associated with foreign educational systems. Under the U.S. Agency for International Development, the combination of "participant training" in the U.S., along with contracts for American universities to supply advisors to foreign universities, has constituted an exchange process with effects similar to the Fulbright program.

Military assistance programs have also generated a stream of trainees coming to the United States. While their programs have often been brief and specific to military specialties, they have added to the role that the U.S. plays as an international educator.

Currently there is a developing momentum for forming direct

linkages between American and foreign universities especially with countries now in a position to move rapidly in university development by virtue of petroleum revenues or other fortuitous new resources. A 1976 survey (Overseas Liaison Committee, 1976) reported that nearly 60 American universities had linkages of one kind or another with Iran alone.

The scale of exchanges has been further enlarged by grants made to American scholars to pursue foreign area research abroad under Title VI of the National Defense Education Act of 1958, an important basis for developing area study centers in the United States. While this has largely supported Americans rather than foreign scholars, it has made a very substantial contribution to projecting the American educational system abroad, and establishing the professional contacts by which the American position has been attained.

EVIDENCE OF THE ASSETS FROM
EDUCATIONAL COOPERATION

Cumulatively, the consequences for communication due to this educator role can be dramatic. The case of Egypt has been particularly striking, for the effects became suddenly evident in the context of renewing official relations with Egypt in 1975. This had come about after a prolonged break and an interval of Soviet presence and influence in various aspects of Egyptian affairs, especially military and development matters. Given the turbulent course of U.S.–Egyptian relationships in the preceding decade, the ease with which a wide range of government-to-government cooperative activities, as well as private ventures, were resumed was impressive—and somewhat surprising, at least to the Americans. It quickly became apparent that part of this was due to the fact that many of the officers in Egyptian ranking ministries, parastatal institutions, planning agencies, and university faculties were American-educated professionals. These were people whose graduate work in the U.S. dated back to the era before the break—that is, before the 1967 war with Israel. Hence, whatever the difference in negotiating position, there was a surviving basic ability to communicate accurately on many technical and managerial issues, an ability to comprehend motivations, and even to empathize. This may have been one of history's most salient cases in which it was demonstrated that a foundation of mutual understanding built through effective educational exchange could directly affect the course of official relations.

A number of elements set this case in bold relief. The amount of educational exchange was substantial. The break in relations was dramatic, with violence against American installations. Deep emotional factors, precipitated by the Israeli war, were involved. And an unfriendly Soviet presence was maintained during much of the interval. Yet several American educational institutions, such as the American University in Cairo and the Cairo American Research center, were able to continue operations through the break. This continuity helped to bridge the break in official relations. It might be noted that the Soviet presence may have enhanced this ultimate reunion for their dour, humorless, guarded, and less-than-open approach did not wear well with the Egyptians, and their economic "cooperation" did not do much to make Egyptian standards of living more tolerable. All of which goes to show that getting people together so they can get to know each other does not always improve the relationship!

Much of the American-oriented educational connection was built up through the Egyptian "Missions" program by which the Government of Egypt sent their eligible scholars abroad to gain Ph.D. degrees in a wide variety of fields. Exact records do not seem to be readily available, as the program apparently began as long ago as the 1920s. But the significant phase which produced the leaders now in place—to effect today's communication with Americans—was the post-World War II flow, which lasted until about 1964. Some 100 new Egyptian scholars entered the program each year, this number increasing in the early 1950s. Thus, approximately 2,000 Egyptians went through the program, and while Egyptian officials claim that about 600 never returned, a large number still did go back to take positions where their training was badly needed. The Fulbright program added to the number, especially between 1964 and 1967 when about 400 received American education by this route.[2] AID also had sponsored about 850 for varied length programs. Others gained degrees from the American Universities in Beirut and Cairo.

This means that a pool of perhaps 3,000 American-trained Egyptians matured professionally during the years of the official break, and many of them were well advanced in position by 1975 when the American relationship was renewed. Some of the American-trained had gone to better paying positions in other parts of the Middle East, and there was competing influence from fraternities of Egyptians who were educated in Europe, or during the break, in Eastern Europe or the USSR. Still, the American linkage was a most important one; one American Fulbright professor working in Egypt in the education field in 1976

[2]Statistics are combined from interviews with several American and Egyptian officials in Cairo, 1976.

reported that of the approximately twenty deans of departments of education in Egypt, all but one or two held U.S. Ph.D.s. Moreover, the effect of American education has spread beyond Egypt because Egyptians staff other universities and educational institutions in the Arabic-speaking Middle East area.

A few other samples might be cited to show the cumulative effect of American educational activity as a basis for effective communication. By 1976 in Indonesia, AID was able to list more than 4,000 Indonesians who had gone to the United States for training programs; USIS listed nearly 1,000 as having been on Fulbright and related travel grants. Military assistance programs had sent about 1,200 in the period after the end of the Sukarno regime, and various foundation grants had added another 500. England had trained about 1,000 in technical fields. With the demand in Indonesia, people with foreign training credentials tended to be placed quickly in responsible positions.

The Philippines presents an even more impressive situation, of course, because of the U.S. presence there since 1900, and the continued special relationship after independence at the end of World War II. The full statistics of public and private educational involvement there can never be compiled; the entire Philippine educational system was under U.S. administration for about 45 years. But even since 1952 some 4,400 Filipinos have received U.S. training under AID programs, and while the "brain drain" may have taken its toll as some have been attracted to better opportunities abroad, many do occupy significant positions at home, and a number have been employed in international agencies. The Fulbright Alumni list for the Philippines numbers about 1,000. The total who have sought U.S. higher education privately exceeds all of this. In 1975, official Philippine figures showed 2,600 Filipinos concurrently studying in the U.S. Today, the largest part of university faculty members with Ph.D. degrees have received them in the U.S. The Philippines, in turn, has become a training center for nationals of other countries in the area. In 1975 there were about 1,800 foreign students at the University of the Philippines alone (Quezon City campus) and substantial numbers elsewhere.

Other countries now also illustrate this educational relationship. Soon after the increase in world petroleum prices (i.e., in 1975 and following) the Venezuelan government decided to send large numbers of students abroad for technical education. Most were sent to the U.S., with numbers reaching the thousands by 1977. Nigeria has stepped up its use of American educational centers, and Iranians now constitute one of the leading nationalities among foreign students, with an estimated 40,000 in the U.S., either officially or privately financed. It will be particularly interesting to see what role these students will play in U.S.–Iranian communication relations as Iran makes the transition from the U.S.-supported government headed by the Shah.

The point of these statistics is that as an ever more standardized technological education becomes a key factor around the globe for producing the goods and services needed by complex societies looking toward modern life, the nation that provides this education rather automatically has a head start in its ability to communicate abroad. This does not mean that all people educated in the U.S. will also automatically yield to the U.S. point of view, or that the same advantage will hold for nontechnological subjects. It does mean that less time will be lost in talking past each other on a number of commonly important subjects, and in trying to capture the logic of an American approach. It also means that many people in other countries will be able to shift intellectually from the context of their own culture to something of an international culture—U.S.-centered to a degree—and to an international set of conventions for transacting business or dealing with technological matters.

THE MOST TRAVELLED PEOPLE

That Americans are the most travelled people on earth is obvious enough, but the fact needs to be stated here because this is an added asset for the American position in the international communication system. This does not mean that the American's presence abroad necessarily enhances the American image, contributes as much to the visiting American's understanding of the world as it might, or increases the desire of others to accept communication leadership. The evidence is very mixed in these regards. But this exposure does allow more Americans at more levels of the society to think in global terms, pursue international activities, and be relatively well-informed.

About 1.5 million Americans reside overseas, including some 400,000 U.S. Government servants or their dependents.[3] Except for international travel in Europe by Europeans, the volume of American tourist travel stands out as an unprecedented circumstance for providing a global perspective. The shortfall in American readiness to think and deal in international terms will be considered in a later chapter, but here we need to note that the sheer international mobility of Americans is a formidable factor. There are in addition millions of Americans who, despite having no desire for foreign travel, nevertheless have had inter-

[3]Estimated from several categories in Department of State statistics, 1978.

national exposure forced upon them by their service in the armed forces. Most of America's warfare, and much of its routine defense activity, has been carried out abroad. Although for many this has been a negative kind of international education, it has produced a different outlook in them than in the case of the veterans of other countries who fought their wars at home with little occasion to cross their own borders.

THE PROBLEM AREAS FOR THE
UNITED STATES

For all the factors that cast the United States as lead actor in the international communication system, and at the same time give it formidable advantages for meeting the responsibilities of that role, some very real problem areas exist. A number of political and psycho-cultural factors tend to undermine the American's otherwise advantageous position, reduce readiness to accept United States initiatives, and create anxieties regarding the effect of a strong American communication position on the rest of the world.

The difficulty posed for Americans is that these problem areas are not so easily seen or appreciated from their own ethnocentric perspective. There is a substantial gap—perhaps a growing one—between the way that Americans see themselves as communicators, and the way that the rest of the world sees them. Here is where trying to gain a certain objective distance from the American scene is worthwhile, for the issues involve parochial outlooks and often strong emotions and preoccupations on all sides; any true picture eludes everyone. Unhappily, too little scientific study has been undertaken, but enough evidence exists at least to note a list of troubling factors which should be taken into account.

The first problem area is found in the reaction to size itself, to the overwhelming American communication position. Psychologically, it is quite different to be on the receiving end of a one-way flow of news, information, education, and popular culture, than it is to be on the creating and sending end. In fact, it is also different to always be on the receiving end of economic assistance or even disaster relief. Americans have little experience in that position, and little preparation to empathize. It is hard to appreciate that the very strength of the American position, however magnanimously utilized, can become a liability. This will be discussed at greater length in Chapter 4.

A second problem, especially in the Third World, is a perceived "guilt by association" with former white colonial powers. This generalized outlook is added to whatever amount of "imperialistic" record the United States has on its own account. In an era when many national groups are hypersensitive to colonialist mentality or activity, it is hard to distinguish the behavior of the United States or of Americans from the colonialist history of their allied Caucasian friends, despite the American self-image as champion of freedom and self-determination. The possibility that some American activity is not in fact very distinguishable is especially hard for Americans to see.

The end result is that what Americans do in a genuine belief of disinterested charity or as a well-intended extension of a helping hand frequently is seen as an attempt to control or co-opt. In Bolivia, for example, where U.S. aid reached some of the highest levels per capita in Latin America, the charge was often made that it was an attempt to capture and control the Bolivian economy for the benefit of the United States. As might be expected, when one tried to counter this with the suggestion (not without its overtones of superiority) that there was little of sufficient economic value to Americans in all Bolivia to match the American investment in Bolivian development, no impression was made. The critics were preprogrammed to suspect the motive and supply their own explanation. Mexico still studiously tries to keep that helping hand at an arm's length.

Critics in developed countries too—France, for example—often take a suspicious view. They also fail to see the special benevolent quality in American motivation that Americans themselves take as an underlying assumption.

Actually, the United States *has* presided over something of a colonial preserve in the Philippines, and from the perspective of much of the world, American hegemony, while perhaps of shorter duration, is of the same mold. Filipino political scientists find wry humor in the accounts of President McKinley dropping to his knees to seek divine guidance in making his decision to impose American administration on the Philippines. As one commented, "How can we complain? It was an act of God!" The status of Puerto Rico, too, appears somewhat more colonial if one looks at it from the vantage point of people living in former British or French colonies. And while technically the U.S. relationship with Latin American countries was not colonialism, the distinction appears greater in American eyes than in those of many more distant observers.

All this readiness to view negatively is compounded by the fact that the United States looms so large in political force, military power, economic control, wealth, and productivity. Almost everyone outside the United States, in greater or lesser degree, feels that he is on a journey with someone else in the driver's seat, and that however nice the driver, or how well-planned the journey, the driver's interests might not coincide with those of all the passengers. It is good to have a giant as your friend, but there is always room for apprehension. If the giant is your enemy, the whole game seems unfair.

This was made clear to me when I was a member of the U.S. Delegation to the 22nd United Nations General Assembly in 1967. The American build-up in men and airpower in Viet Nam was beginning to attract more world attention. Informal reactions around the U.N. seemed to fall into three categories. Members of delegations aligned ideologically against the U.S. were critical, of course; those closely allied in the effort, supportive. But those looking on from greater distance, including friendly colleagues from Canada and North European countries were saying in effect "Yes, we understand that perhaps you have to do it, but our subjective feeling is that it is unfair that so large a power with such overwhelming resources should carry the fight against so small an enemy." There was a sympathy, or at least an empathy, for North Viet Nam that American protagonists at that time felt intolerable.

So, simply being the biggest in a world system is a reaction-provoking position; exercising the responsibilities of bigness, even if done in the most enlightened way, is a psychological liability. Being big and insensitive at the same time would compound the liability.

Then there is the matter of assessing where American credibility and communication leadership stand after Viet Nam, and after a couple of decades of Cold War. Certainly the situation is not the same as it was at the end of World War II, at the height of the Marshall Plan, or in the days when technical assistance was developing momentum. The trouble is that the view Americans have of themselves has not changed very much despite the evidence that Viet Nam did not work out the way they expected, or that Watergate and its attendant domestic turmoil suggest that there may be work to be done at home before the United States prescribes for the world. The inclination to forget Viet Nam rather than pursue what can be learned from the experience is not an advantage for Americans as they look to communication priorities of the future. In fact, even earlier twentieth-century American views of themselves persist, as was demonstrated in reluctance to change views on the Panama Canal.

In any case, a damage report is needed to judge the consequences of years of hostile propaganda plus the cumulative effect of distorted perceptions not necessarily related to the Cold War. To what extent is the United States actually seen as the "imperialist" power that takes advantage and is responsible for the limited economic development of societies around the world? How deeply is this believed? To what extent are minds closed or how mixed are positive and negative views? If one cites the case of Latin America, one would find on the negative side, a combination of hostile propaganda, a widespread marxist—but not necessarily communistic—interpretation of inter-American history and of recent international events, a preoccupation with American "imperialism," and a large-scale frustration with their own attempts at social and economic development. Does all this set the communication relationship with Latin America beyond a point of no return? Have these outlooks been so implanted that they have become the unquestioned assumptions or the conventional wisdom of young adults today, making objectivity improbable in the future? If so, the consequences cannot be ignored, regardless of how favorably Latin Americans adapt to American technology, popular culture, standards of living, and television programs.

Another aspect of the damage report would be a look at the fallout from the way that the U.S. conducted its own side of the Cold War competition. What did this effort, including its excesses, do to United States credibility? How much was lost, for example, in arm-twisting pressure on our allies and others to join us in votes in the U.N. to resist socialist approaches of any kind, to combat reformist movements which were supported in any degree by Communist elements, to maintain unpopular defense expenditures? Or, over the long range, what has been the effect of a prescriptive U.S. moral stance of the kind so championed by John Foster Dulles, that is, the projection of the notion that Americans were best equipped to assess the Communist menace, prescribe a democratic formula, and judge the degree of compliance? Or, from that background, how responsive a chord was struck more recently when Philippine officials, chafing over U.S. criticism regarding human rights matters, charged the U.S. with "moral imperialism?"

I recall that during the height of Cold War fervor a zealot was making the rounds of official Washington with a handy ten-point scale by which one could rate any country in the world in the range between Communism and Democracy. Just check the squares and add the points. Among other uses, he recommended this for troops so that they would have a ready way to judge what they were fighting for. This simplistic patent medicine gained very considerable attention in high places until more analytical minds eased him off the scene. But it was this kind of "leadership" that has undermined overseas confidence in the American grasp of issues as the world underwent vast social and political changes.

Ideological factors and their current relevance, including some more positive aspects, will be taken up in the next chapter. The point here is that there is much evidence that the American holier-than-thou stance was wearing in the first place, and that the Viet Nam reality has left it demolished. Unfortunately, many of today's leaders feel that when they tried to solve real problems in ways which deviated from the American prescription, Americans closed their minds in their attempt to brand everything as good or evil during the Cold War, and consigned them and their efforts to the outer darkness. Such feelings have their lingering effect on the mood of today's communication relationship.

Perhaps symbolic of all this is the paranoia around the world regarding the CIA. When one considers U.S. international strategy in its psychological dimension, it can be argued that whatever the security need for it, the entire CIA activity has been one of the largest miscalculations—or perhaps noncalculations—in America's public diplomacy history. From undermining confidence in its regular diplomatic representation by injecting a CIA presence into it, to eventually naming a former Director of CIA as ambassador to Iran, the United States has demonstrated little sophistication in managing public opinion and perception factors in the foreign affairs process, or even taking them into account. Developing the CIA into a major arm of U.S. policy has failed to consider the gap between the way that Americans see themselves, their intentions, and the justification for their actions, and the way that these are actually understood abroad. It also failed to appreciate just how sensitive a matter this can become in a frame of reference where considerable anxiety already exists about living with so omnipotent a power as the United States, even if it is "morally superior" and gives reassurance of its worthwhile objectives and good intentions. Nor has the whole CIA venture taken into account the peculiarly strategic propaganda advantage this gives to critics by the fact that *it is the United States* that is doing it.

The question is whether the reaction is more negative when the U.S. engages in secret intelligence and espionage activities than when other powers do it. It can be argued, and it is of course, that in the real world all large powers need an effective intelligence service. Most Americans would consider this common sense, and most other people do too—intellectually. And it is realistic to assume that all big powers, given the unpleasant way that the course of events is determined by behind-the-scenes manipulation as well as by surprise tactics and chessplayer strategy, will need the capability to operate in this field. There is also a good case for *accurate* intelligence and clear understandings of the intentions and capabilities of other players in the international arena, for this helps prevent conflict born of miscalculation. In any event, dirty tricks have been around for a long time, at least since the legendary Trojan horse.

The problem is that, somehow, this is not appropriate behavior for the United States! It is inconsistent with proclaimed morality; it is noticed more when the United States engages in it. It more quickly erodes real psychological assets the United States has held in ideological and moral factors which have in fact accounted for much of America's influence since the country was founded on premises that radiated inspiration to many parts of the world.

Hence, the current image of the CIA has to be listed as a distinct liability in United States communication relations. Its activities, or rather the image of its activities, has lent suspicion and reduced effectiveness for a wide range of Americans working overseas: the Peace Corps, the business community, reporters, even priests and missionaries.

The difficulty in looking ahead is that the CIA issue has supplied the sensational kind of copy that sells to mass audiences everywhere, especially where an anti-U.S. persuasion already exists. Therefore, by repetition and intensity of presentation, this facet of U.S. activities stands out in public "understanding" of America far out of proportion to the actual level of operation. It also lends itself to rumor, exaggeration, and distortion, and to being a catchword for blame regardless of what U.S. institution commits an unpopular act. Because anxiety regarding CIA intention and capability has become so much a part of the basis of public perceptions of the U.S., extra astuteness will be required not only to take this into communication calculations, but to avoid exacerbating the liability.

These are not liabilities which, if ignored, will go away. Social scientists who deal with comparative modes of national personality have long noted that Americans are an optimistic people who accentuate the positive, are inclined to see situations in their best light, and are ready to move on to take action on the next problem. So there is a tendency not to brood over mistakes, and in any case it seems unpatriotic to dwell on the negative when the national image is concerned. Yet taking the positive action for which Americans are noted requires making a realistic estimate of the nature of the problem. In this case that means making an objective estimate of the communication liabilities which have accrued, as well as fully recognizing both the real strength of psychological assets special to the United States and the strategic communication position it enjoys.

3

THE DIALOGUE'S
CHANGING SUBSTANCE—
IDEOLOGY, ASSUMPTIONS, IDEAS

Almost by definition, phasing out the Cold War has meant phasing out a confrontation-style dialogue that over the years had become reflex reaction. For Americans this raises the question of where we go from here. For a long time, and especially during the Cold War, America's communication in foreign affairs has stressed ideological concerns, usually in a sense of advocacy and persuasion. Is the United States to continue this role? Does it still have something to advocate? President Carter has tried to take a new hold on ideological leadership by championing human rights. Whatever the fortunes of this initiative, the central fact is that the environment for ideological communication is changing and can be expected to change more. This chapter explores some of the directions of that change.

For purposes, of analysis, the word "ideology" probably is too general; it implies a formal system of beliefs which does not translate easily into everyday communication problems. It is more useful to ask what changes are taking place in the role that ideas, beliefs, values, and implicit assumptions are playing in the international communication process. These aspects of thinking patterns apply directly to the important subject matter that makes up much of international communication: institutions, plans and projects, trade regulations, laws and justice, political affairs, governmental functions and issues. All these are rather abstract subjects; how they are understood is determined by the frames of reference held by those involved in the communication process, and these frames of reference are in turn much affected by differences in

31

ideologies and systems of values and beliefs. The more abstract the subject and the more value-related, the more these cognitive predispositions become significant in debate and discussion. Items like moral behavior, social mobility, human rights, university education, debt obligation, and so forth do not have consistent meanings everywhere. What they mean in any given exchange depends on the set of mind of the speaker and listener, whether at the person-to-person level, or, expanded into international dialogue, at the public-to-public level. Culture and national experience play a large part in determining all this, of course.

A short digression here might help clarify the approach to be used in this chapter. Imagine a professor of communication at the blackboard drawing a simple model of a communication process. Two boxes would represent the "sender" and the "receiver" of messages. Various arrows between the boxes would represent the transmitting process and the complications that affect it—such means of transmitting as speech or writing, mechanical devices used, gestures, feedback, translation problems if the languages are different, distracting noise, etc. Usually when considering the international communication process, attention is directed to the arrows; that is, we consider communication satellites, selective news coverage, translations, and "reaching" the audience—all that goes on *between* sender and receiver. What we fail to consider sufficiently is what is going on *inside the boxes*, or inside the sender and receiver, on each end of the diagram. When individuals communicate within their own society, and especially within their own circle of intimate associates, the content and workings of these boxes are not too different, and differing idea patterns are not likely to pose great difficulties. In this case their knowledge, implicit assumptions, common sense, and conventional wisdom are more or less the same. Like the language they use, these do not need to be taken into account at the conscious level.

However, when the communication is international or cross-cultural, there is a greater probability that these configurations of common sense and conventional wisdom will not equate. Then, like the language, translation is needed if the two sides are not to talk past each other in terms of the real meaning and nuance of their "messages." And it can be argued that much of the time in international dialogue the messages *do* fail to mesh in the cognitive gears on each side, that the participants *are* talking past each other to a greater or lesser degree. Universal thought patterns are hard to come by, and anthropologists find few as they study the hundreds of cultures of mankind. Such matters as religion, social philosophy, ethics, and reciprocal rights and duties of the governed and the governing are particularly subject to cultural relativity. All this is basic to international communication; it is further complicated by change through time and circumstance. Yet very little objective study has been undertaken on the interaction of national belief and value systems and international communication except at the most superficial attitude and information level.

Now let us look to the agenda as America takes stock of its position for communicating values and ideological concerns in an ever more global society. What kind of change is occurring in the arena of ideas and knowledge, in notions of priorities, and in perceptions of international relations? What is going on in the mental "boxes" around the world as the subjects for communication become democracy, free enterprise, human rights, socialism, sharing of basic commodities, economic justice? How much is the American set of mind—changing also—tuned to those of other parts of the world?

As was noted in the last chapter, Americans start out in a highly unique position as an international supplier of ideas, which supplements its already advantageous position in technology, education, popular culture, English language, etc. From its founding years the United States was an experimental country for trying out and digesting new and old belief systems carried from Europe to the New World. Part of John Locke's concept that government is founded on individual freedom and happiness, certain French notions of equality and liberty, English emphasis on doing and on working and self reliance, and post-reformation religious precepts from much of the north of Europe—all were being melded together on the clean slate of a frontier environment. Many other people had a vested interest in noting how the new American ideological experiment was working out. It was all highly visible, and when it was also highly successful the American position in the marketplace of ideas assumed extraordinary proportions.

By the twentieth century the U.S. found itself in a leadership position in the international communication of social values and ideological propositions. American social wisdom had come far toward becoming the conventional, or at least the ideal, model for groups in many parts of the world. It supplied a standard-setting function that has been unparalleled. Other countries copied its constitution, imitated its institutions, accepted its censure, and frequently placed its ideology on a pedestal for comparative purposes. Often intellectuals in other countries could recite more facts and data on American institutional history than Americans could.

Americans have taken enormous self-assurance from this circumstance in conducting their communication abroad. A kind of validated ethnocentricism sustained and gave vigor to the American dialogue. It became the natural rationale and motivation for its role in both World Wars and the foundation for its thrust in the Cold War. It served as an unquestioned mandate for the United States Information Agency to tell

America's story to the world, and it gave both assurance and a special viewpoint to American politicians as they declared their opinions of the foreign scene. The same assurance was fundamental in American intervention abroad in technical and military assistance, business counsel, and advice for political modernization. Also—and this is an important aspect of American international behavior—it imposed a sense of responsibility for compliance with ideals and a need to consider the moral justification for its actions abroad.

The end result has been something of a one-way flow of communication in the moral and ideological dimension, and Americans have come to accept their role in this as a matter of course. The question now is whether in time this role will change, or whether it has already changed faster than Americans have realized. If so, what are the considerations and implications?

THE DECLINING MYSTIQUE OF
THE AMERICAN SOCIAL AND
POLITICAL EXPERIENCE

We have noted, then, the basis for the implicit assumption that America's experience in its social and political evolution should serve as a model and precedent for the rest of the world, and most especially for the developing world, as a model for adoption. Thus Americans have been eager to explain and help others understand how American institutions and democratic processes work. Private citizens and groups have undertaken this task with missionary zeal, and official information activities and educational and cultural exchange programs have been designed and executed with this objective in mind. Other societies were evaluated according to their progress along the path to the American model. And, in fact, this outlook was reciprocated in many places, certainly enough to reinforce the Americans in the logic of their approach.

Now, with world communication relations somewhat in transition, does this model-for-adoption notion still make sense? Americans explicitly carried it into their bicentennial celebration; one series of seminars for which international cooperation was requested inquired into the ways that American experience and culture had impacted on other countries. And when President Carter took over the reins of foreign policy, he reflected this unquestioned assumption. For example, in a speech at Notre Dame University on May 22, 1977, he stated in the context of pursuing human rights observance abroad: "We are confident that democracy's example will be compelling, and so we seek to bring that example closer to those from whom in the past few years we have been separated and who are not yet convinced about the advantages of our kind of life."

Yet, while this approach may have produced some political mileage domestically, it was immediately criticized as naive by a variety of internationally experienced observers (Lefever, 1977). And the pronouncement, if serious, did not match reality when checked out abroad. Again, I will use the evidence of my pilot studies in Southeast Asia, the Middle East, and Africa.

There seemed to be little doubt in these areas that the American model had sustained a certain loss of credibility after the years of its having been heavily promoted, with only limited success, as the solution to social and development problems. Viet Nam, of course, was the most noticeable and publiziced instance in which the model proved nontransferrable. Perhaps it would be more accurate to say that there has been a loss of innocence regarding the feasibility of importing American patterns to solve problems that grow in different cultural soil. There was a declining aura of magic surrounding American institutions as the panacea for developing societies, a decline most apparent in those areas where the politically astute recognized in frustration that attempts to adopt the U.S. model had not resulted in effective government or satisfactory operation of other institutions. This does not mean that the American experience has lost all relevance to them, or that they would turn automatically to opposing models—to, for example, the Communist world. It means that they are now inclined to explore other options. They now recognize that they will need to create their own philosophies and theories of government and their own institutions to meet their special needs. In the short run at least, they are inclined to turn to less-than-democratic governmental practices as a more efficient means of moving from their relatively more traditional and authoritarian societies to what will be their own style of modern society.

The Philippine case is the most disquieting for Americans, given the longstanding efforts by both Americans and Filipinos to make the American model work. It all ended in a long period of martial law after what was reluctantly seen by Filipinos as a near collapse of functioning government. The clear impression given by those watching the scene during that time was that the martial law phase was not simply a temporary expedient but the beginning of a determination by Filipinos to consider a much broader range of possibilities in government and society. A greater degree of authority was considered necessary in one form or another, and it could not be said that the average Filipino citizen was altogether unhappy with this turn of events. The frustration was expressed by one Filipino social scientist long involved in governmental affairs when he applauded the American system of checks and balances, and pointed to their own urgent need for that dimension of government. But he bemoaned the fact that the Philippine Congress—patterned after the American one—had never fulfilled that function, and that, in the light of Philippine political culture, never would.

Most of the countries included in these pilot studies seemed to fit the trend throughout the developing world in that they had relatively authoritarian governments. Yet, even allowing for the improbability that the visitor would be exposed to the full range of dissenting opinion, the conclusion which seemed best supported was that the public was *not* chafing because their governments were less than democratic or because popular participation was less than complete. They were judging their governments rather by the competence and sense of responsibility displayed by authoritarian leaders as they played expected authoritarian roles. Certainly the public was not looking to the U.S. for inspiration for greater democratic practice nor for making critical comparisons as to the direction their own institutions were taking. What they were looking to the U.S. for, and also to other industrialized countries, was technological inspiration, management training, models of production, and styles of modern living.

The comment of a perceptive Filipino perhaps illustrates the trend in a country where the U.S. had always been the first model. He noted that his parents' generation looked to the U.S. for political and institutional inspiration, his own looked to it for professional orientation, and young people today look to it for ways to make money.

In effect, that which Americans tried to promote the hardest in the Cold War era—the theory and practice of democratic society—seems to be of declining interest; and that which they tried to explain away—an image of materialism—is now what attracts foreign interests. For ideology these countries are turning to their own resources.

The implications of this trend for American communication abroad is far reaching. This has been recognized by those with experience on the front lines of communication policy, most especially those officers who, in the U.S. Information Agency, have long advocated a more mature and realistic stance in tune with changing times and needs. But to the extent that a mainstream of Americans carries the lingering assumption that other countries such as the ones referred to above have an inherent and compelling interest in the way that American domestic affairs, institutions, and organizations are working out, some fundamental rethinking is in order. It is not that our foreign audience wants the American model to fail or go away. There is simply a growing sense of detachment and nonrelevance, and therefore a reduction in any real or urgent concern with the way we manage our political processes, campaign for elections, teach civics, or draft labor legislation. They have less reason to identify with the fortunes of American domestic affairs.

It should be observed that while somewhat more attention has been paid here to political institutions, the transplanting of economic ideological systems and basic institutions into another nation's cultural base faces the same difficulties. Communication is affected in parallel fashion. In fact, ideological adjustments in terms of goals and ideal images were made in the economic realm sooner and more pragmatically than in the political. It has been easier perhaps, to see how special local conditions affect economic, than political, organization.

FACTORS IN PROJECTING
AMERICA'S PLURALISM

There is, however, one facet of the American social experience that is of continuing interest, especially in many newly independent nations. That is how America has managed its pluralistic society. Yet there is still a certain mismatch between what Americans think needs to be communicated, and what this audience wants to hear about. Essentially, Americans have been preoccupied by the Cold War competition for attracting the newer nations to the democratic fold. Therefore, sensitive at home to the shortfalls in democratic participation that discrimination against blacks represented, aware that most of the populations of new nations were not Caucasian, and concerned with hostile propaganda that homed in on this American problem, America's projection of its pluralism has come to be primarily a defensive concentration on black–white relations. But for many new nations with a few years experience trying to meld their own multiculturalism into at least a minimally workable national identity, the problems of one group in the U.S.—with whom they do not identify as closely as Americans assume—is less interesting than the comparatively high degree of successful social integration of the total society. They note that in comparison to their own situation, most Americans are Americans first, members of an ethnic group, if any, second.

Perhaps a useful perspective is gained for understanding how Americans are inclined to project their pluralism by considering four facets of it.

First is America as the melting pot, an aspect which much of the world knows about as their own people departed to follow the American dream, usually not to come back. The United States has been a nation of immigrants who by the second generation were integrating into the national society as fast as they could. But the melting pot is history to most

Americans today, and therefore something less likely to be talked about abroad.

Second, there is a quality to its pluralism that results from America being an achieving middle class society, both in theory and in fact, as compared to the rest of the world.[1] Thus ethnic groups, though culturally separate in some respects, generally have had access to the same middle class social ladder. This was not so true for certain groups who felt active discrimination, blacks especially, but as seen from abroad the success that a middle class, achievement-oriented society had in melting separate identities is rather spectacular. The effect in the U.S. has been to reduce the sense that differing styles of living exist across ethnic, occupational, and social class lines. But because this is normal experience to Americans, less conscious effort is made to project it in international dialogue, at least in an articulate way.

Third, there is pluralism as a problem reflected in the American civil rights movement. Here is where the need to attend to pluralism was most forced on American attention. The issue struck all the nerves in the conflict between the American ideal on the one hand—that is, the worth of the individual, his human rights, democracy, equality, justice under law—and the down-to-earth facts, on the other—deep prejudices and the cumulative effects of those prejudices as seen in a subculture of poverty and adaptation to second-class status. The events of the movement were dramatic; they were news, and as such were transmitted to world attention, often out of proportion. It was here that Americans felt most vulnerable in the international ideological debate.

Fourth and finally, there is in America a certain post-Cold War swing away from the melting pot assumptions to the idea that there is some virtue in a multicultural society, a value in building pride and self-confidence in one's separate identity. Perhaps the "black is beautiful" initiative started the trend. It has been applied to education where Chicanos are concerned. In any case, this poses a challenge to America's ability to manage its pluralism: can special identity be dignified and promoted without the danger that the society might disintegrate into a kind of fragmentation politics by which the interests of a national society will take second place to the contending interests of its now more recognized separate parts? As the latest focus of American concern with its pluralism, multiculturalism is being projected into the American's communication abroad.

On balance, it is clear that the third facet mentioned here is the one that has most influenced American international communication.

---

[1]For a recent study of class in America, see Richard Coleman and Lee Rainwater, *Social Standing in America: New Dimensions of Class* (New York: Basic Books, 1978).

Americans have worked with purpose to place the most favorable light on what they saw as the shortfall in their management of pluralism, and that which produced such pain in the ideological conflict. They emphasized progress and tried to refute the distorted criticism. To prove the point, members of minorities, particularly blacks, were put on display as members of official overseas representation and in official cultural presentations. Official visitors to the U.S. were invited to see progress for themselves, with explanations of the problem offered before they were asked for. We sent black ambassadors to Africa and Asia, Americans of Latin descent to Latin America. Blacks were sought out for AID missions and for the Peace Corps.

The question now is whether this might not have been pursued as a disproportionate projection of American preoccupations, guilt feelings, and even with a paranoia which did not match the nonAmerican audience's real concerns or needs for understanding of the U.S. Or at least, in a new international communication environment is it not time to reconsider? It may not have been paranoia. Everyone may have looked as unfavorably on the American treatment of its minorities as many official communicators have feared. But by exploring this matter in the nine countries of the pilot study, it appears that this outlook is partly a misperception, and that probably a major attempt has been made to communicate a message that has not been very important. In the process, a too superficial treatment has been given to that aspect of American pluralism that is more important to many new nations—the basis for its success in achieving such a high degree of national identity. The American is little prepared to understand the full weight of the national identity problems faced by leaders who are trying to achieve enough of a sense of societal cohesion among its citizens to make national government work at all.

Let us consider the African context: some 40 new nations came into existence between 1956 and 1962, almost none of them enjoying cultural homogeneity or traditions of cooperation among local groups. The task of welding together a series of resident tribes with separate cultures and a history of conflict with each other has been much harder than was the American experience of pulling in immigrants who had voluntarily left their native lands to join in a developing American mainstream. It has also been more difficult than integrating today's American minorities into national life—in the U.S. these different minorities presumably want integration, and there is a well-established majority into which they can be integrated. Even the American North–South conflict does little to help American comprehension; it is a century past and is not too parallel a case in any event.

The African problem is compounded by many factors. One is the fact that Africa is made up of what is in effect so many distinct societies. A single country can contain peoples who speak 100 different languages, and who therefore hold more than 100 separate loyalties. Zambian national radio, for example, had to make some hard decisions in selecting as few as ten different languages to be used in broadcasting. Further, the early colonial territorial boundaries which survive to define today's national boundaries were set in large part for colonial convenience—a river, a mountain range, a lake shore. Tribal groups do not necessarily divide that way, so a sense of national identity today is additionally confused.

A second factor is the degree to which tribal social and cultural roots have survived to pervade modern life. Note the following sample situations and instances: national universities, with all their problems of developing as national institutions, have had to contend with the divisive outlooks of their multiethnic student bodies, and faculties as well. The most modern and best educated executives in capital cities lose time from their jobs as they play dual roles; on the one hand they are urban professionals, and on the other they are heads of provincial families whose problems go back to tribal customs and loyalties. One, American educated, was complaining over coffee in the Nairobi Hilton—certainly a center of modernity—about having had to marry his deceased brother's wife when he already had a wife and enough extended family problems. The additional wife greatly complicated his responsibilities back in the province, and reduced the effort and energy he could devote to affairs in the city. At the same time that this conversation took place, intertribal marriages was the feature subject for a national slick-cover women's magazine. Can they succeed? So much to adjust to. To circumcise or not to circumcise? How to repay the bride price if you separate? Will your husband's family accept you, or your own disown you? Religious practices and tribal beliefs do not change quickly. In Zambia the press reported a civil court case in which a widow was seeking compensation for her house, damaged by mob action after she was accused by the defendent of witchcraft. The defense position was that she had, in fact, engaged in witchcraft, and that if the magistrate would come to the village they would prove it.

The press of folk culture is not unique to Africa, of course. Yet its existence in so many varieties in single nations that are in a hurry to form national societies is the inescapable difficulty. It is not conducive to participation in the affairs of modern nations, to say the least. The African political process and sense of national priorities are understandable only in this context. On the one hand, how can you resolve a Kenyan problem, for example, when your constituents are willing to think only of Kikuyu, Luo, or Masai problems? On the other, how in the process of fast modernization do you preserve the tribally-based values which have given meaning to life for the mass of a population?

Thus, while Americans are beginning to talk about a "multiculturalism is beautiful" approach to public policy, African national leaders are looking for ways to downplay group identities. Only in this way can they achieve the necessary sense of belonging to one national loyalty so that Africans, like Americans, see themselves first as Kenyans or Nigerians, and secondly as Kikuyus or Ibos. Fortunately, in some cases African leaders do find that certain traditions and value orientations from tribal culture cut across tribal divisions and can be used to build a moral basis for nationhood. On the symbolic level, tribal dances are elevated to national status in state ceremonial occasions—the late president Kenyatta carried his flywhisk. Kenya has seized on mutual assistance and the cooperative spirit found at the village level in many of Kenya's cultures, and has made of it a national ethic—"harambee." This has enjoyed considerable success. Hundreds of local schools and other facilities now exist because of harambee projects. Tanzania takes the village cooperative ethic further into a value orientation for a socialistic society; Nyerere adopted "ujamaa," the sense of community in tribal life. Kaunda of Zambia is trying to implement a national ideology of "humanism," taken from the idea that the traditional community was a mutual aid society, exploitation was not known, man enjoyed the fellowship of man: "This high valuation of *man* and respect for human dignity which is the legacy of our tradition should not be lost in the new Africa" (Kaunda, 1974).

In all this, the American experience with cultural pluralism can be inspirational, particularly in the successful melting pot and middle class society sense. Africans respond with considerable interest to this aspect of the United States, especially after visits, and seem more inclined to focus on it than on specific shortcomings in black–white relations. (Considerations for perception of the American black will be discussed in Chapter 6.) They apparently would prefer to see the American glass as at least half full rather than half empty, for if the U.S. with 200 years experience still has problems with its minority groups, what are the prospects for ten-year-old countries?

So the more urgent concern for many developing societies coincides with a recognized American forte—its success in making government work in a pluralistic society, one which could have remained much more segmented than it has. Canada comes to mind. From the inside, Americans tend to note what is *not* working well enough; from the outside, it may be easier and more pertinent to see what *is* working. The U.S. experience cannot be ignored. If others cannot generate this psychological base for government and thus achieve citizen participation and cooperation in their multigroup societies, the alternative for establishing the necessary degree of national cohesion is force. This can be done either by authoritarian rule, for which there is often sufficient precedence in the culture, or by revolutionary imposition and then forceful change of the thought patterns of the society as in the cases of China, Cuba, and much earlier, of course, the Soviet Union.

George Ball, in his *Diplomacy for a Crowded World* (1976, pp. 325–6), suggests that the U.S. will be most effective in maintaining its leadership in a "crowded world" if it is able to project its unique and special quality—of which its success in pluralism is a part. He worries that the new emphasis on ethnic identity and fragmentation politics will decrease both the viability of American pluralism and the uniqueness of its moral base for leadership.

Communicating about this pluralism is not easy, however. Two built-in problems have to be overcome. First, Americans have difficulty in articulating the underlying factors which explain the American performance because they are factors of their routine experience and therefore largely out of their awareness, as was noted above. Much of what makes pluralism work in the U.S. is a matter of underlying values and assumptions about the relationship between the individual and the larger group. It is having been socialized in what Almond and Verba (1963) called the "civic culture"—a political culture in which individuals learn to identify with their larger community, state, and nation; come to believe in cooperation and compromise; pay taxes; serve in the armed forces; and feel their membership in a national society as a normal thing regardless of one's separate ethnic or local identity.

Second, it is difficult for those whose socialization has been in an authoritarian and traditional society to perceive what they have not experienced, especially when that which has to be perceived is the pattern of thinking that lies behind the behavior. When one's effective social universe has been the extended family, one locality, or a tribe, it is difficult to appreciate just what the difference in way of thinking is that separates traditional from modern participatory society. In their own ideological framework, this is what the Chinese Communists have tried to do—make ordinary Chinese identify with the well-being of larger collectives of people. Apparently they have achieved some success, but with strong measures which begin in earliest childhood.

The trend that has to be taken into account, then, is this: while there seems to be declining interest overseas in judging the way that America handles its pluralism as a matter of compliance with American democratic, political, and legal processes, there is more interest in approaches for achieving public readiness for effective integration in a national society in the first place.

SHIFTING THE EMPHASIS FROM
POLITICS TO ECONOMICS

With changing times and concerns, and with new issues and events, subject priorities in international communication change. This is to be expected. One of the most significant changes is the change in emphasis that has taken place from political relations to economic relations.

Throughout the post-World War II era, the aspect of international affairs most likely to gain public attention was the political. The news on the front page was more likely to deal with rising or falling governments, elections, or the fortunes of political leaders. Economic news, unless unusually strategic or dramatic, was carried in inside sections. "International relations" as typically interpreted is first concerned with conflicts of political ideology, war and peace, security arrangements, treaty processes, and state visits. When the subject is taught in colleges and universities, the thrust is usually the same. The Cold War, in which a confrontation of political systems was the most obvious factor, reinforced this emphasis. While that confrontation actually was also between economic systems, this facet tended to receive somewhat less attention. Perhaps by habit, the American's concern with political process and political rights at home has been naturally projected into his perception of foreign affairs processes.

In "real life" much of the content of international relations always has been economic, of course. Vast amounts of time and attention have gone into negotiating access to resources and regulating trade, production, tariffs, and finance. But the glamour was in the political field. News reporters and commentators made their reputations and gained prestige by reporting political news. In the U.S. Foreign Service, junior officers sought the political assignments, for that was the image of what diplomacy was all about—they felt more like diplomats when they were in the embassy's political section. Good political officers were more likely to become the Deputy Chiefs of Mission, and best of all, the Ambassadors. The "economic types" were seen as narrower specialists and technicians, people who worked in the shadow of their broader-gauged political colleagues. In a fast moving crisis it was the political officer who was most likely to be at the center of the analyzing, cable-drafting and negotiating.

But this has been changing rapidly, first in the sense of priorities of the international specialists themselves, and now in the public's attention as well. The sheer volume of work that had to go into economic development programs contributed early to that trend. New problems rising out of increasing interdependence appear more urgent than those of political ideology. And the reality of denser populations and a vastly expanded multitude of modern consumers simply changes the function of the international negotiation process and hence the subject matter for discussion and debate. The junior Foreign Service Officer now does opt for the economic cone of the career, and older officers have been signing up for the intensive economics courses at the Foreign Service Institute to retool for economic assignments, for that is where the activity is and where the promotions are earned. Newspaper front pages do carry international economic items. It follows, then, that with the shifting emphasis there is an increased need for reciprocal comprehension of the various patterns of thinking and underlying assumptions that tend to complicate communication about economic matters.

In some respects it would seem that communication in the economic field would be easier than in the political, for it deals with things, resources, measurable quantities. Yet it is apparent that, actually, the discussion will not be very easy to follow for conventional Western notions regarding terms of trade, prices, supply and demand, competition, and most especially the social purpose of economic activity, are being confronted by widely different preconceptions outside the West, and even within Western nations themselves. The potential for misunderstanding in economic affairs is increasing as leaders in nonWestern countries define more clearly for themselves and in their own way what their economic circumstances are, why they are that way, and what their objectives should be. Hence, the debate will become more economic–political and economic–ideological. This is already well established in the communist approach to economics, and is also irreversibly set in the Third World demand for a "new international economic order." All this flies in the face of more traditional economic wisdom regarding systems of finance and production, labor and distribution, relationship of government to economic activity, rights and responsibilities in using international resources, and in conceptions of debts and obligations to assist in development.

Actually, as seen from the pilot studies, two divergent trends stand out that affect the ability to communicate with developing countries about economic matters. One makes it easier, the other more difficult.

The first is possibly the predominant one at the moment. With the need to cope with the world economic system as it is, and with the spread of corporate enterprises that further institutionalize everyone's economic activities on an international basis—the so-called multinational corporations—a large number of people in all countries have a vested interest in joining the system on its own terms, or at least in being able to manage one's domestic business within this reality. Therefore, in the pilot countries many were turning to the U.S. to learn their economics and business practices, if they had not already done so. Or they were relating to economics as defined in England, France, Australia, Japan or a variety of other western European countries, which while often differing to a degree in logic and approach, were still part of a Western system that has been established for many years and now has overwhelming economic assets behind it. Hence, economists and businessmen around the world are trained in Western economic ways; their textbooks come from the West; they join a Western economic culture in business administration, cost accounting, trade promotion and advertising, export–import business practices, banking and credit, and investment analysis. This is being avidly pursued both in private sectors and to a considerable extent in government economic institutions. An article in *Fortune* magazine on Singapore was entitled "Singapore, the Country Run Like a Corporation." Indeed, in all the countries in the pilot sample, from Indonesia to Kenya and Iran, the motivation was great to adapt to the techniques and the rationale of an existing international economy, and to be effective in it. In Southeast Asia, Chinese businessmen, who have much to do with the way the economic system operates throughout the area, are no strangers to the profit motive, free enterprise, industrious application, or international finance. Western businessmen have little trouble communicating with them. Singapore's very existence depends on international trade. Philippine corporations have had to compete directly with American companies on their own soil until the recent end of the Laurel–Langley agreement. Japanese trading companies (and Japanese tourists!) influence economic practices in all parts of that area.

In Africa, both private and state corporations retain expatriates, typically English and French citizens who have stayed on after colonial status ended to help assure that African enterprises can operate in an effective way and compete in the Western-based international economic system. Iranian corporations used to recruit them in substantial numbers. Latin American business leaders have often been educated in the United States or through their experience in foreign companies operating in Latin America. Often there are not enough of them: as the supply of Brazilian managers has failed to meet the extraordinary demands of the Brazilian economy, substantial numbers of Americans have been imported—at a lower cost than hiring Brazilians—something of a come-down for the Americans!

In short, there is a considerable vested interest in much of the developing world, as well as on the part of their business mentors in the West, in speaking the same language in economic affairs and in operating on the Western world's own terms. This tide has strong impetus and support. It is part of the trend toward a degree of internationalized culture mentioned in Chapter 2 and it constitutes one of the most important channels in the entire range of international communication.

But there is a counter-trend of growing importance, one that will impose a much more difficult task in mutual understanding. The Indonesian case would illustrate what is involved. In 1975, then Secretary of State Henry Kissinger made a speech in Kansas City in which he argued that the present international system had served the world well. Not only did that statement draw widespread attention in Indonesia, but the dissenting reaction was immediate even though this is not an area that displays the strident protest and rhetoric of "exploitation" found in other areas (such as in parts of Latin America or Africa). Yet Indonesia does identify with Third World concerns, and its political leaders, the politically articulate, and much of the larger society are looking for more adequate formulas to gain more of their own social and economic objectives than they see coming their way in Secretary Kissinger's present world system. Leaders in Indonesia did not feel strong pressure from their constitutents to meet *political* participation needs, but they did feel the heat to meet *economic* participations needs, in both the domestic and international economies. The Indonesian public was suspicious of foreign leverage or advantage. The multinational corporation was the subject of growing, if still low-keyed, concern, with little knowledge displayed, but with a distinct sense of threat to national sovereignty and a fear of being used as pawns as companies were suspected of moving operations from one country to another to keep wages low. Prices for raw commodities, terms of trade, maintaining control over investors, and protecting local industry were all issues which competed for public attention, along with such domestic problems as controlling the private economic abuses of their own political opportunists. The much-publicized Tanaka riots of 1973 were generated by this combination—a reaction to what was seen as overbearing Japanese economic leverage in Indonesia plus political protest against Indonesian leadership, which was believed to have sold out to this leverage.

This, then, is one kind of counter-trend. As the reader well knows, it can be seen in much of the Third World and is reflected in international discussion, from the halls of the United Nations to editorial comment in the most obscure and provincial newspaper. It is a pattern of economic logic developing from the view of the world seen from inside these countries. It is a function of nationalism, a memory of colonial history, a local preoccupation with development, and a localized view of the international economic process and its distribution of benefits. Sometimes this is lumped together as the "north–south confrontation." In any case, this is where the strain will be felt in communicating on economic issues and where a real difference exists as to what makes "common sense" in economics. As more coherent philosophies of economic priorities and social needs are devised in these areas, the communication problem will become more complicated. More diverse patterns of reasoning will contend to establish the meaning of the messages that flow in international economic dialogue.

IDEOLOGICAL COMMUNICATION
AFTER THE COLD WAR

At least in the short run in the post-Cold War era, it appears that communication on political ideology will be less passionate; there already is less prescriptive zeal from both the East and the West. Looking ahead, some of the more salient factors which most probably will affect the course of future ideological dialogue might be summarized as follows:

1. With the end of the cold war phase, *there is less of a sense of ideological competition,* less implication of an either–or choice between communistic and democratic systems as defined by the U.S. and the U.S.S.R. There is more disenchantment with the idea of adopting one or another foreign utopian system. Moreover, there is new sophistication on the part of leaders in the new nations—as, for example, in the pilot study countries. Categorizing a country as "underdeveloped" does not necessarily mean that the decision-making elite is "underdeveloped." Perhaps such leadership is in short supply, or reaches its decisions in the style of local culture and within existing constraints. But it is increasingly competent in conceptualizing the reality of its own society, in setting priorities, in thinking through ideological considerations, and in choosing what is needed both from internal efforts and from foreign assistance. Most important, these leaders are more determined to take the responsibility for setting the direction of their own development, more wary of deferring to the counsel of foreign advisors however well intentioned, and are saying more clearly, in effect, "We will be the ones to decide the way in which our institutions will develop."

Longer-established nations as well feel less compulsion to align themselves with one world model or another as their political, economic and social systems are undergoing change almost as traumatic as that in the developing world. There is more inclination to experiment and adapt in ideological approaches to resolve the problems specific to their circumstances. England is an example; Italy, Spain, and Portugal are others. Readjustments are pragmatically made in the Communist world, including both the U.S.S.R.—now more than 60 years a Communist nation—and the People's Republic of China.

All this is part of the trend: attention to one's own logic of government and society, borrowing political ideas on a pragmatic basis, and feeling less sense of ideological competition in making the choices and decisions.

2. *Changing demographic reality calls for some updated assumptions about the nature of government and its proper function.* Viewed sociologically, this simply means that a different kind of governmental function must be supplied when populations are more dense and when more specific coordination of everyone's activity is required if the social needs of all the society are to be met, than would be the case of a sparsely settled and infrequently interacting society. Government plays a different role in a settled town than in a nomadic tribe, and still another in a modern urban society. More tasks have to be accomplished by the society for the society—disease control, for example, or welfare for the aged. More specialists are needed, and government becomes more technical and impersonal. When one adds that demographic changes include trends toward larger, more educated, communicating, and consuming middle sectors, and that these groups are losing their patience in developing societies, the pressure on government performance and delivery is serious indeed. Government has to become a more efficient, tightly operated, more encompassing operation. Resources require strict management. There is little margin for slippage, less leeway for allowing individual independence and choice. There is less social room for individual elbow-stretching—a trend also seen in the United States. In any case, the ideological notions born on the American frontier, which are already having to be redefined in the United States itself, will have ever less relevance in other countries as they feel the need for government coordination in ever more aspects of public and even private life. American ability to communicate in a global society which is moving in this direction will require a much less ethnocentric set of lenses.

3. *Preferences will continue to shift to more socialistic approaches to meet social objectives* and away from free enterprise assumptions implicit in long-standing American ideology. This will be true also in the United States. The question will be what kind of socialism, and to what extent traditional Western values will be preserved. Part of the reason is the demographic factor described above, yet part also is the fact that many new nations reflect traditional values which tend to place emphasis more on the group and less on the individual. If one starts with the assumption that the group is central, that the individual receives his identity from the group, and that his well-being is an aspect of group well-being, many

ideological matters—law, social justice, human rights, and the role of government in the society—will will be seen in a different light. Hence, it seems more "natural" in many societies to opt for more collective approaches. So far Americans have given the impression that they will suffer democratic socialism but not encourage it. Much deeper understanding of the forces and ideas involved will be needed if the American side of ideological dialogue is to be relevant and constructive. In any event, the United States needs to be sure that the image it projects in this regard is not that of its most conservative and doctrinaire minority.

4. At least in the short range, *preferences will continue toward more authoritarian governments.* The dilemma is that in order *not* to need tight control by government when populations are dense and a lot of discipline and coordination are required to meet pressing social objectives, a high degree of civic culture—that is, built-in restraint and sense of cooperation for the common good—must be available. If it is not already there, it can not be easily or quickly developed. Even such an advanced and civilized nation as Argentina feels this. India went through a phase in which it argued forthrightly that India could not afford the luxury of *not* being authoritarian. The view, for better or worse, is that the needs of the total society for security, coordinated management of resources and production of goods and services, welfare, directed social change for a mass subsistence-level part of the society, and all the other requirements for achieving modernization and staving off revolution are so urgent that the nation cannot afford to leave the process to chance—which freedom of individual and group action is seen to represent. The difficulty is that the problems of modernization are those that have to be resolved at the national level of society at least, and probably, in this era of interdependence, in coordination with other nations as well. Therefore, while it may be preferable to allow greater freedom, and the freer societies of the West are held in esteem, the prospects for progress in desperate circumstances seem better if less of the common purpose is lost in the contention of opposition political parties, through an undisciplined press, or by individual license to exploit advantages at the expense of the collective effort.

This does not mean a preference for the caudillo-type dictatorship of Latin America or anything like it. It means, in many areas, stricter authority resting on a popular base and reflecting social purpose. There remains the recognized need to discipline those who wield the discipline, to maintain a sense of social purpose on the part of those who hold the advantage within the authoritarian system. Still, experiments in attempting progress through less authoritarian means have left frustration, and the publics of a number of nations seem to prefer benevolent authority over democratic processes in their own conception of their self-interest. The Philippines seems to be such a case despite the great lengths Americans went to to put all the institutions, laws and procedures of democratic government in place. What Americans did not successfully implant was the civic culture to go with it. Consequently, it did not work very well. Now Philippine leaders are trying stronger measures, and the Philippine public is, from all the evidence, adjusting more easily than we would expect. They do worry about abuse of the new authority, the lack of restraints, and the evidence that the use of much of this authority is directed toward privileged personal advantage rather than the greater social progress.

Communist regimes add their own ideology to this basic assumption about the need for authority to coordinate social behavior. Then they go further to try to change the political culture as quickly as possible, to build into the individual's values and thought processes a sense of identity with the larger society's interest. It is in the excesses of their methods, as well as in their specific objectives, that Westerners see human values violated. Yet one of the appeals of Communism seems to be that it gives those who hold no advantage anyway a feeling that there *is* a public policy that will cut through the chaotic hodgepodge of narrow vested interest inherited in the course of uncoordinated social change, and produce a society in which they will have more of a share. It is not too hard to give up doing your own thing when you never had the means to do it anyway, or serious expectation that you ever could.

The attempt to get the individual to identify with the larger group's purposes is illustrated in this vignette. An American of Chinese ancestry recently went back to China to visit her friends and relatives of pre-Communist high school days. In the old days, she remembered, if someone tried to get off a streetcar without paying his fare, the other passengers would remain carefully uninvolved. It was a problem for the conductor, and none of their business. But when that happened during her visit to the People's Republic, everyone on the streetcar got into the act and scolded the culprit for his unsocial behavior. If this was as spontaneous as it appeared it would represent a substantial change in some of the basics of political culture.

The problem posed for American international communication, then, is that it is probable that many publics will choose more authoritarianism in government than Americans would consider natural. Thus, the Americans will be faced with less audience interest in their championing of individual freedom than they expect. Perhaps the outlook is ambivalent—if one could *go* to the United States and participate in the freer society, this freedom would be preferable. But in certain social realities, many might see their own vested interest best advanced in a combination of authority and enlightened social purpose.

5. Whether it be considered a factor in ideological communication or not, one of the salient values which America projects is its mass high standard of living. *The trend in much of the developing world, at least among planners, is toward more modest and realistic aspirations.* An Egyptian official, for example, stated that it was impossible for him and his colleagues to be effective if they held up the standard of living of the West as their serious objective. AID officers have reported the same pragmatic realization on the part of responsible planners in most of the places where they work. They consider the outlook sound enough, and have molded much of their assistance effort to fit more attainable goals determined in cooperation with their counterparts. The point is, however, that there is a gap between the expectations the American public would pose as the standard for progress around the world, and the expectations of the elites who must make the decisions and set the rationale for their development activities. As this acceptable gap becomes better articulated in the Third World, not only will the American good life decline as an asset in American communication abroad, but it will be seen negatively—as an impediment to other nations reaching even their more modest goals. Thus the high standard of living that Americans project abroad, both intentionally and in the course of normal communication processes, may come to undermine their leadership position in cross-ideological dialogue. This trend is quite evident already.

The value placed on constant expansion, on the bigger-is-better objective, is being questioned in the developed part of the world too, of course. A trend seems to be well established toward more consideration of the "limits to growth," for the "small is beautiful" concept, zero growth, and controlled consumption and new lifestyles that respond to limits on resources and the trouble that threatens if more equitable use of these resources is not managed.

IDEOLOGICAL COMMUNICATION
AND NATIONAL SECURITY

The importance of the way in which Americans relate to the ideological debate in a more global society can hardly be overestimated. Continued advocacy of ideological positions which are losing their synchronization with the concerns of the rest of the world, or are even out of tune with those at home, will produce little more than a pleasant stroking of American egos. American leadership in the realm of purposes and social values, of ideas and moral implications, has an important function to serve in a more global society. The U.S. is still a world resource for such, and it is looked to for playing that role. And, given the American position in the flow of communication, if it does not exercise that leadership, it is less likely to be provided by other Western nations.

It can also be argued that rather uniquely, American security depends on its ability to be effective in its ideological communication relations. Security depends to a great extent today on alliances and on performance within these alliances. This, in turn, depends on the *will* to ally, the sense of common purpose, a public sense of comfortableness in an identity with the United States and its objectives. Confidence is a substantial security asset.

All these are very subjective factors; ones not easily quantified and included in the models by which one measures national power and influence. However, there is a perspective here that needs to be actively pursued, for so much energy and attention goes into the highly technical aspects of the planning that surrounds budgets for defense, weapons systems, military assistance, and the arrangements for multilateral defense operations that the motivational base on which all this revolves is left uncritically assumed. The case of Iran is a painful reminder. Ultimately the question is who actually *uses* military capabilities, and when, under what circumstances, toward what objectives, and with what degree of determination. Today it is last ditch security if a nation has to go it alone, so it is essential to consider the public psychological cement that holds alliances together. Alliances based on fear, short range economic advantage, or pragmatism in a given crisis or regarding a given issue do not promise much sustained security for its members. Even within a nation, national power and effectiveness depend on social cohesion and consensus on objectives and means. When international cooperation is the key to accomplishment, mutual values and a deeply felt sense of common purpose are a source of strength for which there is no credible substitute. This factor on both the domestic and international level has been evident in its presence in both World Wars, and its absence in Viet Nam.

As evidence of the reality of a relationship between security and these psychological factors, the stated justification for a long list of American decisions in military matters has been the need to maintain *credibility*. By this we usually mean maintaining the image of U.S. power and willingness to use it, our projected sense of commitment to promises and agreements, or some combination. But in the context of this discussion, one suspects that we often use a very narrow conception of credibility.

Throughout modern history, America's strength has rested heavily on its projection of values that have struck responsive chords in other people's sentiments and goals. Nations joined the U.S. cause, or invited American participation in their causes in part because their publics *wanted* to ally themselves with what the U.S. represented—not simply because of American military or economic capabilities. Thus, although it is much harder to bring these factors to the surface so that they can be examined and taken into account, there is a compelling logic for looking ahead to the psychological dimension of security. This means looking to the ideological communication process and responding to trends that are taking place in it. Unfortunately, objective research, and even the ability to conceptualize this "soft" side of international relations, is woefully behind the sophisticated analytical tools that are directed toward management of the hardware and command structures which go with modern defense operations.

4

DILEMMAS POSED BY A ONE-WAY FLOW
OF NEWS, INFORMATION
AND POPULAR CULTURE

When the first astronaut stepped onto the surface of the moon, I was in Cochabamba, Bolivia, a city not very far from the high Andean altiplano that looked pretty much like the moon itself. There was no television to carry the historic event, only the Voice of America being rebroadcast through local radio stations, backed by the wireless ticker in the back of our nondescript United States Information Service Office. But the landing still created a lot of excitement. Science students displayed the models they had built of the lunar landing module. USIS set up a large make-believe television set at the corner of the local plaza, using a movie projector from behind to show films from previous rocket launchings. It attracted large crowds all day. There was wide discussion and anticipation. Some never believed it was really happening at all; it was just another clever American science fiction program. The more credulous speculated on the nature of outer space and the engineering problems of jet propulsion. When the landing was successful, I found myself something of an instant celebrity as the ranking American in town. There were phone calls from local officials and well-wishers, and demands for a word, live from Cochabamba, for the radio audience.

It did not take much imagination to put oneself in the Cochabambinos' place and feel a bit of wistfulness in their outlook. For all their fascination with the dramatic exploit, it was not *their* event. They were, as usual, on the receiving end of important events taking place somewhere else. They were being informed essentially through the all-powerful channels of American information facilities about American happenings. One could empathize with the attempt to retain self-dignity when a few intellectuals assumed a rather studied I-can-take-it-or-leave-it stance. As it turned out, those responsible for public affairs planning for the moon venture had also empathized. They downplayed the American initiative and genius in the coverage, and pointed to the many scientific discoveries by people of many nations which led to the successful achievement—they proclaimed it a milestone for mankind. At first I felt this was a bit transparent. But that approach was warmly received, and I found myself repeating it with conviction in carrying out my own public relations responsibilities in my remote corner of the foreign audience.

This small slice of international communication is suggestive of the larger issue posed for the United States. Although the global aspect of society is becoming ever more apparent, a heavy one-way flow of news, information, and popular culture will persist for a long time given the Western, and especially the American, position as the most advanced information society, and the sheer momentum of its international communications enterprise. How does the United States, in decent respect for the opinions of mankind and a mature sense of its responsibility as an international communicator, strike a balance between pursuing its own legitimate communication interests and at the same time being responsive to the difficulties that the one-way flow poses for many other nations?

This is an extraordinarily difficult question because "the United States" is not a monolithic solitary actor in its international communication, and never can be. For by its fundamental principles, communication, whether within or without the society, is an area which is intended to be regulated at a minimal level. Thus, no matter how wise, well-informed, and concerned the government, American communication behavior internationally is a composite of a vast array of essentially untamable communicators. Government can define the issue, lead and even control a certain important part of America's communicating abroad, but the nation's overall behavior will be determined at a much more public level. This is what frustrates those who must deal with the U.S. in these matters—there is no place to grab hold and insist.

If there is any accuracy in describing the world condition as "interdependent," it certainly applies to communication: to its production, its channels of transmission, and most of all its consequences. Few people can remain immune to the ripple effects of other people's communication activities short of isolation by force.

For those able to compete with some degree of self-assurance, the process can be more straightforward and even satisfying. To wit, one evening on British television David Frost, the British media entrepreneur who had conducted the much publicized post-Watergate Nixon interviews, was hosting an interview with the Prince of Wales, presumably the next king of England. As the show opened, Prince Charles stated with mock seriousness that he wished to assure the television audience that "I am not a crook!" This would seem to be interdependent television at its finest.

But much of the world has more experience being *dependent* rather than interdependent in its international communication. This has gone on for a long time, and the effects have been cumulative. Now the reaction is gaining volume, often being expressed in ways that reflect more frustration and emotional response perhaps than rational search for solutions: "cultural imperialism," "information imperialism," "picture-tube imperialism," and demands for a "new international information order." Censorship and restrictions on foreign newsmen are being imposed more frequently as a defensive mechanism and a protection from the onslaught of foreign culture and values whether or not there are political reasons in addition. Nonaligned countries are consulting among themselves and are mutually reinforcing their positions. UNESCO has been extensively engaged in the debate over the right to control information that crosses national borders, a matter to which we will return in this chapter.[1]

What are the psychological forces at work in a one-way flow? In the first chapter it was suggested that because Americans have little experience at being on the receiving end, they are slow to anticipate the psychological reactions generated by being in that situation. This subject is beginning to attract attention now as a proper direction of inquiry, particularly in relation to extending assistance, and even charity and disaster relief. It has been pointed out, for instance, that in the mid-1970s India went out of her way to purchase grain from the Soviet Union to meet emergency needs rather than go the assistance-from-the-U.S. route that had become so demeaning to self-esteem. In the process, the Russians had to make unexpected purchases from the U.S., and the price of bread went up for American housewives.

Psychologists Kenneth and Mary Gergen report that their research demonstrates that recipients view assistance with perceptions considerably different from those of the agencies that extend it.[2] Motives are questioned, the morality of receiving it is rationalized—it is repayment for exploitation in the first place. There are logical reasons why there

[1]For a collection of articles which presents a range of views and concerns surrounding the issues involved, see Kaarle Nordenstreng and Herbert I. Shiller (eds.), *National Sovereignty and International Communication*. (Norwood, New Jersey: Ablex Publishing Corporation, 1979).

[2]For an accessible summary, see Kenneth and Mary Gergen, "What Other Nations Hear When the Eagle Screams," *Psychology Today* (June 1974, p. 53).

would be less gratefulness expressed than the donors would consider appropriate. Anthropoligist Wilton Dillon in his book *Gifts and Nations* (1968) noted that all societies have patterns of giving, receiving, and *repaying* gifts. His data led him to the conclusion that some of the running negativism on the part of the French toward the U.S. after the Marshall Plan was due to the disruption in this set of customs. Americans extended help with great generosity but did not want anything that was French in return. A satisfying and dignified reciprocity was frustrated; thankfulness turned to resentment partly because of the position in which the French were placed.

A similar psychological factor may be considered in relation to the one-way flow of news and information, entertainment and popular culture. The fact of being on the impotent side of the flow would have psychological meaning in itself. At the minimum, any judgment as to the consequences of the flow on the recipient society would have to take into account a different reasoning process than that of the American communicator. One man's modern television entertainment might be another man's attack on his culture and values.

This chapter, then, is concerned with two general areas in which imbalance, and the way that difficulties growing out of imbalance are resolved will affect the quality of future communication relationships. The first will deal with the press and the flow of news, and the second, will make a brief exploration of the very broad field of the media, with an emphasis on television and popular culture. This leaves out many important considerations, for example, the American's need for a reverse flow of information to increase his own competence to live in a more interconnected world. That will be taken up in some detail in the last chapter.

Also left out here, despite its fundamental importance, is the set of international public policy problems surrounding Western supremacy in telecommunications equipment and technology and the difficulties the international community must face in regulating and managing the staggering array of new communications possibilities now on the horizon. All this will come to a focus in the 1979 World Administrative Radio Conference in Geneva, which will be the controlling one for the next decade. Not only is policy debate demanding on this issue because of the technological, defense, and economic contentions that these space age wonders pose, but also because the imbalance in advantage between have and have-not nations adds an additional dimension of contention. One of the first of these issues to stir political debate was the prospect of direct satellite television broadcasting—the potential to beam TV programming from the vantage point of space directly to home receivers. In the principle of freedom of information flow, the United States championed an open skies policy. But there was little hope that this would be seen benignly; the U.S. advantage was all too apparent. When the issue of regulation came to a vote in 1972 in the U.N. General Assembly, the U.S. found itself in a minority of one against 102.

As every nation's security and economic viability comes to depend more and more on access to communication channels, anxiety regarding the advantageous American supremacy grows. Already Americans are contracting to place communications satellites in orbit for other nations as it is the U.S. that has the efficient means to do it. Americans control much of the resources for transmitting messages through the strong positions of ITT, ATT, RCA, and by the INTELSAT arrangement. The Soviet Union is the nearest competitor. Consequently, those who do not want to tie their communications fortunes to the Soviet sphere of influence are left with the U.S. as the choice patron. But much more than simply sending messages is involved. The ever more significant computer-assisted storage and retrieval of information, and computer terminals for preprogrammed data processing, are tied into the telecommunications system. International use is made of a wide assortment of computer nerve centers and information repositories, from the *New York Times* data bank to medical diagnostic terminals. Financial transactions of all kinds travel the telecommunications and computer processing route. No international corporation or military organization could pretend to modernized operations without these resources.

Yet, while intimately related and highly important both in itself and for perspective, this area is a somewhat different subject and will not be pursued here. It is being effectively researched elsewhere, is debated in such international forums as the meetings of the International Institute of Communications, and is the focus of an increasing amount of literature.[3]

AT ISSUE: IMBALANCE IN
INTERNATIONAL NEWS FLOW

Except perhaps for the messages that go back and forth between governments, the flow of news stands out as having the most significant consequences of any element in the entire international

[3]For example, Ithiel de Sola Pool at MIT and Anthony Oettinger at Harvard have been salient in this field. I have also profited from Wilson Dizard's syllabus and review of literature prepared for a course on "Communications, Information, and National Security" at the National Defense University, 1977–78. The Communication Institute at the East–West Center in Honolulu has advanced the inquiry in the Asian area, and a wide assortment of studies has been generated in preparation for the 1979 World Administrative Radio Conference in Geneva.

communication system. Such factors as just what is chosen as "news," how it is interpreted and conceptualized, to whom is it disseminated, and how credibly it is received *determine the data base* for interacting in international society. It becomes part of the fundamental "knowledge"— whether accurate and complete or not—by which the psychological processes of the mind turn out perceptions, judgments, reactions, and decisions. It is to international life as the city newsroom is to community affairs; possibly it is more significant, for a local community has more alternative ways to know about local affairs.

The first problem is what becomes news. Whether by objective initiative, accident, or design, some events rise above the attention threshold to become international news; others are left dormant. Over time, the chosen news contributes to images held of countries and their leaders, of foreign peoples and their ways of life. And, for televised news, images are produced very quickly. It is never possible to report every event or the full context in which news occurs. There is always a selective factor, and therefore a possible distortion in the public understanding. Through much of the first half of the 1970s, Viet Nam was front-page news—for several years thereafter, it rarely was. It is not that events had stopped taking place there, but the reporters were not there. No reporters, no events. A minor matter gets more attention on a slow news day. Politicians pray that they will make their errors on days when reporters are busy elsewhere and the front page and the fifteen-minute newscast is otherwise preempted.

It is precisely this selective news gathering and processing that is increasingly at issue. As journalists, reporters, and news managers perform one of the most important functions in an ever more global society, the term "gatekeeper," used so often in communications studies, is especially appropriate. The importance of how they do their job can hardly be overestimated.

Nations with the strongest news institutions and a head-start in the technical means of transmitting news, and which also have a strong vested interest in consuming news, are easily in the best position to determine what the news is and to whom it should be available. It has been this way for a long time, and like other facts of life in international affairs, it has been accepted as a normal attribute of national power and influence. But now with the vastly increased flow and penetration of news, publics that had never had reason to consider how their own events fared in international news coverage are feeling the feedback effects, and the system *is* being contested. There is rapidly mounting concern about imbalance in the flow, about the "right to communicate," and about the disadvantages of being beholden to the news giants.

Statistics are not needed to convince the reader that the Western world, and especially the United States, enjoys the advantage. It is obvious enough and no extended account will be attempted here as the subject is discussed in other sources.[4] Still, a few illustrative items are impressive. For example, when it comes to access to the channels for transmitting information, more than one hundred countries or territories are leasing services from the U.S.-dominated INTELSAT. International Telephone and Telegraph (ITT) has become almost symbolic of the American advantage. It stands highly visible, with operations in over 60 countries and more than 400,000 employees. Even the newsprint on which the world press depends is essentially a production monopoly of the First World.

More familiar to the layman is the position that the large news services command in international news flow. Associated Press and United Press International stand out as being by far the most important in packaging news for world consumption. Add the British-based Reuters and Agence France-Presse, and the lion's share of news processing is accounted for. Other agencies, including the Russian TASS, remain as minor or too specialized to play an important part in the way the international community get its news. Associated Press is a cooperative of 1,350 member newspapers with an organization which employs 2,500 journalists and supplies services to more than 100 countries. UPI sells its commercial service to some 2,000 subscribers outside the U.S.; it operates more than 200 bureaus in 62 countries.

From around the turn of the century until World War I, it was Reuters that informed the world with its base in London where the international cable system converged. It is still the basic service for many countries of the former British colonial empire, as is Agence France-Presse for the Francophone world, although the latter is a distinctly smaller operation. Both are significant additional channels in the international news network.

The American news weeklies *Newsweek* and *Time* are found on newsstands in cities in most world regions. It takes an appreciable portion of their cover pages just to list the local newsstand prices for each country in a sales region. Much of the specialized news that deals with international affairs issues is supplied through the New York Times News Service and the Washington Post–Los Angeles Times News Service, or appears in Europe in the *International Herald Tribune*. The *Times* of London has been influential, again taking advantage of the growing utility of English language materials. *Le Monde* is a centerpiece in the

[4]Two notable sources are William H. Read, *America's Mass Media Merchants* (Baltimore: Johns Hopkins University Press, 1976), and Jeremy Tunstall, *The Media Are American* (New York: Columbia University Press, 1977). Some of the general data in this section comes from these sources plus Dizard, cited in Footnote 2.

French-speaking world. Major economic events are covered by such Western or Westernized sources as the *London Economist* or the *Far Eastern Economic Review*.

Yet the printed newspaper may not be the way most people get their news today. Radio, and increasingly television, carry the load for mass audiences. Still, electronic news is based largely on the same news services, and although it is a more flexible medium inviting local choice and variation on the text, the one-way flow in selecting and defining what the international news is to be is a basic reality. To this must be added the long radio arms of international broadcasting services, and also the reach of stations close to national boundaries: Canadians listen to American stations, for example. The British Broadcasting Corporation is heard around the world and is relied on by a substantial number of out-of-the-way elites. The Voice of America provides news service in as many as 32 languages. Radio Liberty and Radio Free Europe operate in the European area. And when you tune your short wave dial you also get the Western word from Radio Canada and Radio Netherlands, along with various other less extensive national services. One of the radio and television news sources which is little studied but probably is of competing significance is the American Forces broadcast service intended for a U.S. military audience based around the world. As others have tuned in too, this presence often has posed problems for host governments or for competing stations. The cases of Iran and Japan come to mind, as well as countries of Western Europe.

Imbalance in news flow, and the question of whether the American sense of news priorities matches needs elsewhere, have become matters of increasing anxiety in much of the world, particularly in the Third World. This disquiet is now being translated into action at an ever more determined pace. At first it was the subject of occasional nonaligned world conferences meeting in the early 1970s in places like Algiers, Lima, Tunis, Mexico City, New Delhi, and Colombo. Among with providing a forum for expressing indignation, the aspiration was to establish a choice in news sources, to set up nonaligned news pools or regional news agencies. Much of this discussion took place within a UNESCO framework. One result was that Yugoslavia took the initiative to offer its government-owned news agency *Tanjug* as the facility for a nonaligned news pool.

The issue made much more impact on world attention when it came up in a more insistent and politicized form in the UNESCO General Conference held in Nairobi in 1976. Soviet influence in confronting Western nations with what was called a "draft declaration on fundamental principles governing the use of the mass media in strengthening peace and international understanding and in combating war, propaganda, racism and apartheid" spurred a determined reaction when it became apparent that the intent was to establish the principle that states should have the right to "correct" news and to control the international flow of news as it affected their own media. The threat to press freedom and to the free flow of information was obvious. This fire was brought under control with an adopted resolution that called for a more balanced flow of information in the Third World, but with the obvious step gained that "imbalance" was to be the subject of much more careful attention by all parties.[5]

Continuing attempts by countries feeling the "imbalance" to do something have posed new problems for Western newsmen, and have spurred counter-complaints that the principle of free flow of news and information that seemed to have been universally accepted outside the Communist world is being negated. Some of this complaint has been particularly insistent when Western newsmen have been denied access to cover news events in the Third World, as in the case of civil conflict in Nigeria, or when news has been censored in previously open countries—a growing trend.[6] They have spoken out when the civil rights of foreign newsmen have been curtailed, as in the case of Percy Qobozo in South Africa in 1977, or in the assasination in 1978 of the leading opposition news editor in Nicaragua, Pedro Jaoquin Chamorro. The World Press Freedom Committee, an American initiated organization but one also supported by European and Asian membership, has taken the lead in articulating the threat. News managers began to discuss the growing problem more often; Western governments grew more worried.

By the time that the next UNESCO conference convened in Geneva in the fall of 1978, more people on all sides had had their attention called to the issues involved and to the need for a more constructive approach to the imbalance problem. In particular, Western leaders in the international news field, along with government officials, came to recognize that Third World complaints were not simply the mischief of the Communist bloc or the tail-twisting sport of formerly colonial areas. Real problems were being generated by the imbalance. In any case much of what was being proposed to create regional news pools, to better news facilities among Third World countries, or to strengthen

---

[5]A background analysis of these developments is contained in a report prepared by the Academy for Educational Development, The United States and the Debate on the World "Information Order" (Washington: Academy for Educational Development, 1978). For a synopsis, see Jonathan F. Gunter, "An Introduction to the Great Debate," *Journal of Communication* (Autumn, 1978, pp. 142–156).

[6]For further discussion see Mort Rosenblum, "Reporting from the Third World," *Foreign Affairs,* July, 1977. (Vol. 55, No. 4, pp. 815–835.)

capabilities for development journalism was not necessarily a threat to the West's interests in news management. And among an increased circle of those from Third World news institutions, the disadvantages of controls became more evident as they projected the consequences as related to their own relative advantage.

All this permitted a higher quality of groundwork to be carried out before the Geneva session. Once convened, Ambassador John Reinhardt, leader of the American delegation and also director of the International Communication Agency, signaled a problem-solving mood by formally recognizing the need for attention to growing Third World needs and by offering U.S. assistance in supporting regional training centers, providing more access to information resources, and further cooperation on the technological front.

Behind-the-scenes discussion and maneuvering were intense, but in the end the conference bought time for developing cooperation and for more studied approaches in addressing issues and needs. The principle of free flow in international news was preserved; the West gave assurance that their serious attention had been established. The imbalance issue had not been laid to rest, of course, but the stage of sterile confrontation seemed to have been passed.

It can be expected that all this will be the subject of much further rhetoric, hopefully of responsible analysis, and certainly of a lot of negotiation. Our purpose here is to examine underlying communication factors and their trends. What, basically, is the argument all about?[7]

One of the first complaints by those dependent on the Western press is the one already mentioned—that international issues are selected, defined, and conceptualized for them without their having much input in the process. The items in international negotiation that receive the most publicity become the key issues. Personalities gain power by press attention, or they are deprived of international position without it. It was reported in 1978 that then President of Venezuela Carlos Andres Perez found from a poll of U.S. public opinion which he had commissioned that the vast majority of Americans had never heard of him, and did not even know where his country was located. This was just before President Carter was to visit Venezuela.

That which is of interest to Western news consumers must, by economy of scale, be assumed to be of interest to everyone. That which is not of interest to the mass of Western clients is not news. Critics feel that the news is inevitably slanted to mesh with the world view as seen through the Western lens by which news is processed. For example, an

---

[7]Part of the following observations has been enhanced by my participation in the New York Conference on the Third World and Press Freedom, 1977. For substance, see Philip C. Horton (ed.), *The Third World and Press Freedom* (New York: Praeger, 1978).

Indonesian noted that when the U.S. presence in Viet Nam precipitously ended, that country had "fallen." He agreed with the conceptualization, actually, but complained that he was not given the choice. Disparaging and approving terms are used by reporters everywhere: leftist, imperialist, graft-ridden, democratic, progressive. Those who control the news get to use their favorite adjectives more often. The Japanese complain that while they try to accurately refer to their military activity as "Ground Self-Defense Forces," the international press converts this into "army," implying that the Japanese are defying their own constitution which prohibits an army.

A second aspect of news dependency is that there is little news service between and among Third World countries with similar problems and interests. One African country gets news of its neighbor through London or Paris; Latin American news makes its way through New York. This is painful to colonial memories, which is reason enough to provoke nationalistic sentiments. When the substance itself does not seem to reflect a Third World sense of news priorities or context, the frustration grows. The large news services counter that their objectivity and quality *do* reflect professional journalistic standards, and that their services *are* designed to serve regional needs out of proportion to profit and loss considerations.

Perhaps the most fundamental issue revolves around the social purpose to be served by news institutions. Sometimes the purpose is quite apparent, as in the case of Soviet pronouncements or in the Third World stress on "development news." More often it is not as explicitly recognizable; in international debate there often are differences in underlying assumptions about the function of news flow in a society. Note the following contrasting frames of reference.

There is a Western "ideal" conception. This is that news is the objective reporting of events to give the public the basic knowledge that will allow it to be informed and arrive at opinions. What effect the news will have is not the criteria for its selection; if it is a meaningful event, it should be known. As the "fourth estate," the journalistic establishment is a necessary supporting pillar of a democratic society, a part of the checks-and-balances system by which a people can in fact be in charge of their own government and make intelligent choices. It assumes the public's right to know. Therefore, news must flow freely, and news institutions must be free of government control, or the control of vested interests, that would preclude the press from exercising its professional responsibilities. In the best of all possible journalistic worlds, there would be no national differences in professionalism, and something like the medical doctor's Hipocratic oath could apply to news reporting.

Then there is the Western view that news is a commercial product.

This is the "common sense" side of the news business in the West, but it is not a point usually made by Americans in their international dialogue, except to advance the claim that news can thus be free from government support and therefore free from government control. It is considered a normal aspect of the free enterprise system. But this is not so "normal" to all observers. To some it explains why the news actually functions as it does in the Western system and suggests that the profit motive might not serve the social purposes of all those dependent on today's one-way flow. In baldest terms, this commercial view is that the news worth reporting is that which sells to news consumers. If it does not sell—if no one is interested enough to pay for it—then it is not paying its own way and its fate has to be left to the professional or altruistic motivations of the press establishment.

Profit is, of course, the basis for operating the international news services, either directly for the services themselves or indirectly as those who buy the service intend to sell it to their subscribers. (AP is technically a nonprofit cooperative.) To the communist critic, this predictably would be interpreted as denying freedom for the press—the press must serve its master, that is, the client who can pay. To the Third World this commercial mechanism for meeting a societal need is troublesome also. In their point of view, business interest control can be as threatening as government control, and if news is a commodity to buy and sell, then they are at a disadvantage because they do not present a market with the strength to determine news selection. They feel that they buy news packages designed first to meet someone else's financially stronger demands. They see their worst fears realized when news is combined with advertising, and, as in the case of TV, when it is admittedly presented in form and style to deliver the largest audience to the advertiser who pays the cost of the newscast. From this they feel that it is only a short step for news to become entertainment, and that actually this is the purpose that is often served by news from their own areas. Their bad news, that which appears bizarre in the West, and the violent event are all emphasized often in a patronizing way, and become raw material for American entertainment even though presented as news. That the same process may take place in the West's own domestic selection of human interest and feature stories does not seem to take away the sting.

In the Third World there is the view that news is a *strategic resource* for national economic and social development. When development holds the highest priority and there is a short supply of competent reporters, of printing or radio equipment, newsprint, and paying customers, then there is a reasonable argument that these resources must be carefully husbanded to serve the most pressing social needs: education, national cohesion, technical competence, morale in national identity, and popular support for a government that probably will not be able to meet the rising expectations of its public no matter how dedicated it is. This, then, is the concept of *development news*. The reality for much of the Third World is that this emphasis also means that it becomes the responsibility of government to support the news establishment, and exercise some control over it. Given this conception and the enormity of the development task, news values that might have been inherited from the West readily change. While a free flow of news and the facility to express individual opinion is theoretically desirable, there are not enough news resources anyway, and news that fosters disruption or reduces confidence in government or its agencies is seen as an added burden that may overload a fragile system.[8]

Giving priority to development news generates a considerable ambivalence in the minds of Western observers. Obviously communication is an essential tool of development, and development is a proper objective. There is sympathy for the fact that the problems are great and the resources few. Without some stability, cohesion, and predictability, Third World development efforts will be dissipated. So the Western news establishment comes to support development news as a legitimate social function in a nation's communication activities. But the dangers stand out for those who also value democratic society. The line is thin beyond which managing the news becomes thought control, and the individual is reduced in his dignity and rights to be a manipulated cipher in a development equation—or worse, if government is less than benevolent or competent.

Thus, the debate comes down to a closer look at the free press concept, and what it comes to mean in differing societies and cultures. To make a comparative analysis, it must be recalled that the concept in its ideal form in the Western democracies includes notions of professionalism in journalism, an educated public that uses news against a substantial knowledge base, competing sources of news, and protection against libel or a blatantly irresponsible press. If one is accustomed to thinking of press freedom from the vantage point of a civic culture in which objectivity is a virtue and the press has ethical and professional standards, it is difficult to appreciate the frustration in societies where this tradition is not part of the culture, where press freedom in fact has often become press license. Here we see the ambivalence for the Third World. In tune with the aspirations that go with modernization, a free press is a popular objective. But the prerequisite qualities of culture which would support a fully socially responsible free press in an ideal

---

[8]For one moderate statement, see Narinder Aggarwala, "Press Freedom: A Third World View," *Exchange* (Winter, 1978).

manner are missing. Therefore, the "free" press has not always been all that attractive.

Latin America may reflect some of this ambivalence. The free press is held high as a symbol of the democratic ideal, and in fact a number of news organizations have developed in the best international tradition. When the press has not been restricted, the number of publications has been large. But closer observation shows a different and more down-to-earth practice. Few of the hundreds of newspapers that have been published in Latin America have been economically viable. They have never made the profit that assures independence, or their reporters and staff professional salaries. The analysis has to pursue further questions: Why *are* they published? What function do they actually provide? How does the reporter actually make a living? In effect, many newspapers—and radio stations too—must depend on the person or group that can subsidize them. They may supply a prestige or an ego function; they can be the information arms of political cliques; they might be worth their cost as instruments of power. Newsmen may have patrons; their incomes then will depend on what they choose to print—and not to print. The point is not that the Latin American press establishment has a pragmatic and perhaps opportunistic quality unique to its area. These facets might be found to greater or lesser degree in many places, including the United States. But when a press operates both freely and without real responsibility in a society in which certain prerequisites of social and political culture are missing, press freedom can come to mean something quite different than the ideal Western conception. Hence, a purposeful government may conclude that a free press is a luxury it cannot afford. In the short run at least, the checks and balances are not there. "Freedom" translates into disproportionate individual advantage at the expense of the larger social objective.

A case in which these two contrasting views of press freedom have hung in balance most vividly was that of India during the last years of the Indira Gandhi regime. The free press tradition was strong, but in the special sense that the Indian press had developed as an instrument of the Nationalist movement, not out of the full tradition of the British press. The Gandhi administration argued that the press had to exercise restraint in its prerogatives in the interest of national cohesion of purpose in development, that full press freedom too often resulted in irresponsible dissipation of the national energy. When the elections turned the Gandhi government out, the Indian press again operated on the basis of its own sense of priorities and considerable professionalism, but one suspects that the contest may not yet be over.

Not surprisingly, this difference in conception as to how beholden the news establishment should be to government affects the way that newsmen and new managers look at themselves. To Western newsmen, independence is a badge of honor; their loyalty, at least in their formal system of values, is to the profession, and this applies vis-a-vis government both at home and abroad. In fact, they project this orientation into a notion of universal professionalism; they judge their foreign colleagues accordingly. But in the Third World, loyalties are more mixed. Many journalists do work closely with the international press, perhaps were trained in Western journalism, and identify with that international fraternity—at least part of the time. But they also feel their special social function as newsmen in societies undergoing rapid change. They inevitably are more political as they are advocates or critics. Their situations force on them more committed roles, a greater association with causes. The elite structures of their countries do not provide room for the neutral and objective observer of events and trends. They may be on a government payroll, or they may be looking to that status in the next government if their cause should prosper. The difference is not categorical; there are many individual variations. Still, there is a patterned distinction to be made, and the Third World newsman can be expected to resist the pretensions of the First World journalist who tries to serve as the conscience for the entire international fraternity on matters of press freedom and independence from government.

A further complaint regarding imbalance in news coverage is that when Western reporters cover events in Third World countries, the news is too regularly distorted and reported out of context, and images are projected which are unfairly unfavorable. Or, if the reporters do a good job, their editors in the news services do not. The bad news of disaster or incompetent performance that attracts attention in the all-powerful international news channels gets out of perspective, especially when the reader or viewer has little other means of forming impressions of the Third World country in question. The frustration is the greater because Third World "good news" does not sell in the First World. Further, it is felt that most Western reporters are culturally insensitive, ignorant, or both, and that as they make crash visits to cover those events that do rise above the threshold of international news interest, they do not gain the meaning and local nuance that is needed for an accurate understanding. Thus, the pressure grows to limit the access of foreign reporters, and the desire increases to project one's own news. That this is unacceptable to the large news services adds to the standoff and to the sense of news "imperialism" noted above.

When one projects this trend of growing concern regarding imbalance into the future, the issue may come to be expressed in more philosophical terms. Western communicators most probably will need to address their attention to an idea that just now is in the take-off stage.

This is "the right to communicate." The context here is a mulling over of the modern meaning of the United Nations 1948 Universal Declaration of Human Rights. Is there a human "right" to communicate? This has a different connotation than simply freedom of information. It implies a right to have access to the system in order to impart information, to give feedback, enjoy a two-way flow, and possibly the right *not* to receive communication if one does not want to. It is a questioning of what might be thought of as an existing laissez faire international communication system, at least as it has grown up around Western initiative and expanding technology. Has freedom of flow in fact resulted in inequality in access and advantage both within nations and in the international system? And in the process, is there now a "right to communicate" that has to be considered in the value system of a more global society?

This discussion was started by Jean d'Arcy in 1969 in calling attention to the implications that the revolution in communication technology would have for the social and legal arrangements by which the world would use these new wonders. The discussion has gone through widening circles in international conferences, UNESCO debate, and an increasing amount of literature. Recent work at the University of Hawaii and at the East–West Center in Honolulu has pulled some of the various threads of this debate together so that it is now somewhat easier to see a pattern to the concern.[9]

The "right to communicate" may become a meaningful issue within the United States in due course. But internationally, it is now an idea that is directed essentially against the position that U.S. communicators enjoy through existing freedom of news and information. This would appear to be a sample of the form that ideological debate will take in a more interdependent world in which overall ideological systems will not be so much in contention as the assumptions and values that go with resolving specific issues that rise from increasing interconnectedness.

THE PERVADING INFLUENCE OF
AMERICAN POPULAR CULTURE

That American popular culture is making a profound impact around the world hardly needs stressing. Like news imbalance problems, the cultural impact is often aired in UNESCO forums, and even more

---

[9]See L. S. Harms, Jim Richstad and Kathleen A. Kie (eds.), *Right to Communicate: Collected Papers* (Honolulu: University of Hawaii Press, 1977). This also contains the Jean d'Arcy article which first appeared in the *EBU Review*, 118 (1969, pp. 14–18). An expanded set of papers is contained in L. S. Harms and Jim Richstad (eds.), *Evolving Perspectives on the Right to Communicate* (Honolulu: East–West Center, East–West Communication Institute, 1977).

broadly at the public level. American movies and their stars have probably changed foreign cultures at least as much as automobiles and electricity. Popular music and blue jeans are in high demand even in the Soviet Union. The TV series Bonanza has been prime tube fare almost everywhere television has reached. *Readers Digest* sells 12 million copies a month in 22 foreign countries, and is translated in 13 languages. American advertising firms have branch offices around the world. In 1978 Coca-Cola marched into the Peoples Republic of China several steps ahead of an American ambassador. American comic strips apparently survive the translation gap from Japan to Turkey. An Indonesian educator commented that the single most important force for social change in his country was the presence of American teenagers; the second was the Indonesian teenager who had been abroad. Singapore cancelled its youth exchange under the American Field Service when the impact on Singapore seemed too threatening. American sports have mass appeal abroad: Mexico is taking up American football, Japan has long been proficient in baseball, and Taiwan tends to win in the International Little League. Businessmen around the world are taking up golf (not exactly an American invention) as part of their internationalized executive culture. The Japanese have even installed driving ranges with a system of nets on the top of buildings to allow pursuit of the golf craze in a space-hungry land.

Some of the impact is not immediately obvious, but nevertheless far-reaching in consequence. Role expectations are frequently cited. Exposure to foreign media can suggest new ideas of self-identity and patterns of behavior for teenagers, women, students, factory workers, even businessmen and executives. Sometimes this aids adaptation to modern life. Sometimes it creates severe strains and personality dysfunction.

This is a vast process. A few notes regarding its analysis might be helpful as a framework. As a start, I suggest that what we are observing is the largest scale *acculturation process* taking place in human history. And communication is the essence of its momentum. This is where the idea that we are caught up in a developing "global society" is analytically fruitful, for it is in this larger context that these social and cultural movements make the most sense, and where the heavy one-way flow produces its most profound consequences.

Sociologists and anthropologists have long been concerned with the interaction of cultures, and the effect that one culture can have on another. When communication was limited, the cultural traits of one society might diffuse to another, as cultivation of the potato moved from the Bolivian altiplano to Ireland, or the rifle came to the American Indians. With closer contact and more intense communication, the borrowing and sharing of customs and artifacts became the cause of more far-reaching social change, as people adapted and rearranged their life styles to accommodate the new patterns that had become a part of their lives. A multinational corporation's new factory near a peasant village, a tourist hotel in Bali or Pago Pago, the American Army in Germany—these are unavoidable acculturation situations. One culture rubs off on another, or perhaps on each other. Now that travel and communication have reached the scale that they have, the acculturation process has stepped up exponentially. And the range of cultural items brought into the process has also broadened to include virtually all facets of life. Thus has come the impact of what we have called American popular culture: it is the driving force in very rapid social and cultural change everywhere.

The big factor in the acculturation process, of course, is the mass media. It is the vehicle by which popular culture reaches the mainstream of populations. And the big factor in the mass media is rapidly coming to be television; it already is producing profound effects in the industrialized world and is growing rapidly in the other world areas. It is revolutionary in that it adds sight to sound, and by mass production of receivers vastly multiplies the kind of impact movies have already produced.

Of course, the movies' influence has not gone away. Movies are still highly important in affecting social change, although the American predominance of the post-World War II years has given way to a more internationalized film industry. Indeed, many "American" films are now made in Italy and Japan, and India is now one of the world's largest film producers. The range in quality and in the images and ideas that films portray is as broad as imagination and public gullibility will sustain—and that is very broad indeed![10]

What actual effect all this has on the cognitive processes of the people exposed to it defies any reliable study, and such analyses as have been made are fragmentary. Certainly in observing movie audiences in my own assorted travels, sometimes as anthropologist and sometimes as diplomat, differences in probable effect seem apparent. It was one thing to watch audience reaction to a Barbra Streisand film like *Funny Girl* in a cosmopolitan movie house Ipanema in suburban Rio de Janeiro, and another when similar first-run movies eventually reached the local cinema in my more provincial temporary home town of Cochabamba, Bolivia. By way of further contrast, I paused one evening during a stroll around the central green as the crowd gathered for a movie in Indonesia's Ujung Pandang—the old city of Makassar in the Celebes that recalls the romantic novels of sailing ships and the spice trade. The film obviously was a lurid combination of violence and stereotyped jet set adventure; it appeared to be an American film, although it most probably was produced in Japan. Certainly the admission price was low

---

[10]Again see Jeremy Tunstall's *The Media Are American*.

enough, and the audience was going to be a big group of young viewers. What would they perceive in the film? How would it affect their own pattern of Indonesian values and interests? How would it affect their image of the United States? One could only speculate.

It is something of an eye-opening experience for a thoughtful American to attend an American movie in a place where he is the only American in an audience of people whose actual experience in the United States is nil, whose understanding of American life will come from movies and related assorted windows onto American society. The movie content typically is not designed to inform, but to entertain an *American* audience. Some particularly low quality films are produced for export in the first place, produced on the basis of what will sell in places like Ujung Pandang. Again, they are not very helpful for mutual understanding. The American movie itself has changed in recent years, with great implications for the impressions they create overseas when seen out of context by foreign audiences. They probably present a much more distorted and hard to comprehend image than did the cheap gangster and cowboy movies of an earlier period. From the American "counterculture," changing sexual mores are reflected; abnormal pseudopsychological themes and new and more imaginative forms of violence have become standard. Specialists worry enough about the social impact on American society itself; it is hard to even estimate what it does to mass audiences elsewhere. This is acculturation in its most frightening form!

Happily, there has been a brighter side to cultural sharing via movies since *The Great Train Robbery* was produced in 1903. The great American films, joined by those of Great Britain and other quality producers, have united international audiences in artistic and documentary experiences that have served as more positive bases for building a common entertainment culture. Stars like Charlie Chaplin, John Wayne, Greer Garson, Clark Gable, Elizabeth Taylor, and Alec Guinness are already global society figures.

But now it is movies *and television* with its capacity for instantaneous transmission of media events from sports to coronations, from exhortations of world leaders to warfare. Films are more cumbersome. They have to be developed, transported, and shown in selected places. It is television's ability to bring the world and its events visually into the living room that produces a new era in international communication. And the nation with the greatest resources holds the communication advantage; it selects the subject material and the nuance of its presentation. Because television programming began in the United States and enjoys economy of scale in its American audience, the one-way flow has been heavily from the United States outward.

Television also differs from movies in its built-in continuing demand for program material. Once broadcasting is established, there are hours that must be filled, and American resources have been ample and available as foreign television stations started their operation with a bare minimum of locally available material, or even the capacity to produce it. American products also provided quality beyond the capacity of early foreign producers. Therefore, while the 1960's high tide of U.S. export has probably passed, in the early 1970s the U.S. still supplied as much as 50% of television time in many Latin American and Middle Eastern countries, and a third in some European countries. (A more exhaustive review of this is available in Jeremy Tunstall's *The Media are American* and William Read's *America's Mass Media Merchants.*)

Television's acculturation impact, and the implications of a one-way flow will become more significant as television in many countries, and especially in the Third World, expands from serving its present small and already internationally sophisticated urban audience to reach mass audiences. The one-way popular culture impact has already been clearly recognized—and reacted to—as to the potential for direct satellite broadcasting to home receivers has become apparent. It is threateningly clear that by this technology Americans, with their belief in the free flow of information, their upper hand on the satellites, and their programming capabilities, could leapfrog the program plans of local governments and broadcasters to reach audiences at will. As already noted, in debates in international telecommunications conferences this has been seen as just too much freedom, and the U.S. has been overwhelmingly outvoted on this front. But whether by direct transmission or by its momentum and overpowering capacity, Western television will be the source to contend with, and the issue is raised for many countries: what is the social purpose of television, and who will control it?

In countries where television is just beginning to expand to public dimensions, concerned leaders are acutely aware that managing the TV monster will be a challenge. They note that it is an issue even in the United States. There the evidence is mounting that long hours before the tube have affected children's performance in schools, that constant exposure to violence has had adverse consequences in personality formation. Foreign leaders also hear the complaint that commercialized television has so reduced the potential for quality programming that a frustrated public is turning to alternatives in public and cable services. The question presses—how to domesticate the beast, and to what end?

The Indonesian case illustrates the dilemma. Its first satellite is now in operation, enabling a network to reach all of the 2,000-mile island chain. How do you fill the hours? To repeat the approach that has been used elsewhere and simply fill the time with *I Love Lucy* or its equivalent does not seem to be the way to bring Indonesian villagers into modernization. In fact, severe limitation has already been imposed on the amount and kind of foreign material that can be used. But it takes time to develop quality local programming, and the urban viewing public is quickly dissatisfied. They are not happy in Nairobi either, where tribal dancing fills a lot of program time in the interest of promoting local culture. Those with broader tastes complain that the hours are endlessly filled with people jumping up and down. Nevertheless, the possibility of using television for public education, for promoting national identity, preserving cultural values, and maintaining political support seems such a valuable resource that planners hate to waste any of it.

Several international efforts have been made to help developing countries gear up for the use of television in the development process. The East–West Center and its Communication Institute and the United Nations Development Program have been active. India's recent work in preparing materials for transmission via satellite to inexpensive ground stations in order to reach rural populations has gained considerable attention. This was done in cooperation with the United States, when its AT-6 satellite was available for experimental purposes. Virtually all developing countries are looking to television capabilities for public education; exploring the techniques is an area of major international cooperation.

Thus are the defenses being set up against imported foreign TV programming. Whether for nationalistic, moral, development priority, or industry protectionist reasons, the one-way flow is meeting resistance. Sometimes the local community itself is wary of TV's effect. In 1974 when I revisited a small town in western Mexico where I had lived and conducted research on cultural change the 1950s, I could see that television had just arrived—a few antennas were sprouting from the wealthier rooftops. But the men did not like what they were seeing happen at home. They said that their wives were spending hours watching the *novelas,* getting ideas from Mexico City and abroad, and shirking their household duties! Even Canada has decided to establish a 30% limit on foreign program time as it finds that Canada, like Mexico, is "so far from God and so close to the United States."

On the other hand, television export is not always so negative a problem in this vast acculturation process. It can be a positive factor in international education. It brings news more directly and more realistically to viewers than ever before. It increases awareness that people live in a world of other cultures and patterns of concerns. Children now have more opportunity to understand the world. The documentary has expanded its audience many fold as it has gone from the constraints of motion picture film to videotape. And television technology has many applications beyond broadcasting, as in video cassettes. It can even be put to work to facilitate the acculturation process itself in cross-cultural education. I recall a 20-minute morning show on a Japanese television station intended for English-speaking viewers trying to learn to communicate with Japanese. The entire program, with dramatized illustrations, was devoted to one word: "sumimasen," which apparently did not mean exactly "pardon me," or "excuse me," or "I'm sorry," but an intricate combination that varied with the social situation and the event. Thus, while getting dressed or eating breakfast, one was given a high-quality introduction to the logic of Japanese social relationships and concepts of polite behavior.

While the media, especially news, movies, and television, stand out for world attention as a one-way flow, other factors contribute to American influence in the ongoing and all-pervading acculturation process. Popular culture flows by other channels too, and brief mention might add perspective to the overall picture. One item would be popular literature—books, paperbacks, and magazines beyond the *Readers Digest* already mentioned. Fashion, home decoration, current science, mechanics, and sports magazines get around or are copied in style and content. In Europe, where English readership is substantial, American items enjoy a wide circulation. In many places paperback books and magazines have a second-hand circulation—watch for them when you visit public markets, even open-air markets. The stalls at which they are bought and sold substitute for public libraries, and by appearances, many items seem to have been "checked out" a number of times.

Finally, there is the presence of large numbers of Americans resident abroad. As noted earlier estimates range around 1.5 million, although many of these technically U.S. citizens may have ethnic origins in their place of overseas residence. The U.S. Government alone is responsible for some 400,000 people abroad when families are included. In general, Americans do not change their lifestyles more than is absolutely necessary when overseas, so they present a direct one-way flow of Americana in the acculturation process, sometimes establishing entire communities as islands in the sea of local culture. There are even retirement communities, as around the Lake Chapala area in Mexico.

Some of the greatest shock waves of acculturation have resulted from the presence of American armed forces. American popular culture is injected with the strength of military efficiency as military personnel demand goods and services to suit American standards, local help that is trained to do things the American way, recreation, local housing, even opportunities to exercise an American bent for charitable activities and community good deeds. Forces in occupation status have made the greatest impact, so much so in some places that the local society has faced grave problems in coping with the cultural disruption that has followed.

Okinawa, Thailand, Japan, Italy, and Germany come to mind. The social and cultural impact of moving armies is the story of history, of course. But the point here is that in recent decades, the American armed forces have been the most mobile and have tended to carry the most of their culture, especially popular culture, with them. Therefore, their impact in one-way flow adds to the already strong current. One of the more bizarre repercussions of American military presence—and departure— is the cargo cult of New Guinea. The American bases there drastically disrupted primitive lives. But local people came to like it, so with the Americans gone, a quasi-religion has developed based on the notion that some day the big cargo planes will return, and with them good times again.

Increasingly in many countries there is public introspection and debate as to what is happening to the local society and its integration and values—and what should happen. This is particularly evident in Japan where it is the theme in a large volume of writing appearing in journals and magazines, and in novels and motion pictures. France makes a patriotic crusade out of protecting French culture. Puerto Rico looks to reviving some of its already battered culture.

From the pilot studies it was evident that a first tactic in the interest of rational cultural change was to avoid being simply passive receptors and try to be selective as to the foreign influences that should be encouraged or discouraged. For example, this could be a determination to control what technical and educational assistance is to be sought, which young professionals should study overseas, and in what fields. (This will be discussed further in the next chapter.) Negatively, the tactic can be censorship, directly or indirectly, as in selective allocation of foreign exchange for imports, including media imports. In all the pilot study countries, the government controlled the radio and television networks at least to some degree, and often some of the newspapers as well.

However, public attitudes regarding being protected from foreign influence varied according to position and outlook within the society. We noted earlier that in their desire to be modern and enjoy the amenities of modernization, a substantial part of urban populations, including some of the new middle classes, identify with what they see as the international and cosmopolitan good life. In sociological terms, their "reference group" is made up of foreign and modern people whom they would emulate. For them, access to the stream of communication from the U.S. and Europe is essential. The more, the better; to be up-to-date on fashions and popular music and to live in contemporary style gives them greater social standing among their peers. They see locally produced "Culture" as inferior, and nationalistic attempts to promote the indigenous as tedious.

Another group outlook would be that of the concerned nationalists who do identify with their own society, and who want modernization, but modernization that will provide a constructive sense of national identity and cultural continuity rather than the social disruption and moral vacuum threatened by rapid change. These are the planners, the intellectual elite, the educators, often those close to government decision-making. They need modern communication for their own development, and indeed look to communication technology to move their own masses along in family planning, basic education, agricultural techniques, health care. They want communication from abroad, but they are concerned with the consequences for their society. They, then, are the ones trying to gain some kind of control over what otherwise is a media onslaught determined by the whims of access to audiences, audience toleration, and commercial considerations.

Then there is the segment whose reactions are set by nationalistic or ideological and political reaction to the flow of popular culture simply because it does come from the United States and its allied Western "imperialist" powers. Here there are many variations in perception and motivation. The foreign influence is exploitation; it is thought control and an attempt to maintain domination; it competes unfairly with local talent and resources. It is bad simply because it is alien. This is standard grist for the communist and radical left mill, as Americans abroad know so well. But it does have an appreciable propagandistic and symbolic potential in places where, in frustration, people are looking for scapegoats or for some circumstance to blame for the discontents of their situation. However rational or irrational these notions may be, their potential for persuasion is great, and they are not subject to measured argument or objective facts.

Is there a desire to reverse the flow, to project more of one's own culture into the international melting pot? The basic outlook reflected in the pilot study countries was that a one-way flow is taken for granted in the relationship between developed and developing societies. It was seen as a fact of life when one is on the receiving end. The problem was how to manage that circumstance. Planners tended to place low priority on seeking reverse flow in communication. Usually they were too busy to try to be involved themselves—they were not eager to go on speaking tours or spend their time trying to help educate Americans in the ways of their own culture.

But the more experienced planners do think about problems inherent in their own routine communication in the international community and this has implications for cultural exchange programs. For example, in discussions with them, or about them, it was pointed out that it is difficult to attain a "balanced" relationship when one side lacks self-assurance in its own international competence and sophistication, or feels that its own developing national accomplishments have not yet reached the stage to make real exchange credible. Occasionally there are complaints about participating in conferences which include Indians. Their English is so much better that it intimidates, so the Indians dominate the discussion. Well-travelled Indonesians noted further that their colleagues have a task in learning how to participate in international meetings. There is a cross-cultural problem in setting aside their stylistic and traditional images of formal meetings and social situations and entering into the kind of give-and-take that goes with a modern style of intellectual exchange. They say, for example, that real communication comes from the heart rather than from the mind. Japanese, for all their modernity, report similar problems.

Middle-range leaders often feel awkward when they are invited to the West on visitor grants or similar subsidized arrangements. They have to find ways to handle their sensitivity to an unequal relationship, and their anxiety in being singled out and therefore compromised in some degree either by being identified with a foreign government or by taking on a continuing obligation. They would prefer at least to make their foreign visits in groups, better yet in international groups, where they feel they are among peers rather than stuck in an embarrassing sponsor–client, competent–less-competent, or rich man–poor man atmosphere. An increased self-assurance and sense of security in one's own national identity seems to be essential to a more mature and balanced communication relationship in international gatherings. This is a subtle but very real factor to be taken into account as international conferences and business meetings become increasingly important in conducting world affairs. It is even argued that anything that more established Westerners can do to promote self-assurance for their counterparts will enhance prospects for effective exchange and cooperation.

Would not this objective be advanced if in an increased flow of reverse communication more attention could be focused on the traditional culture and achievement of the developing countries, allowing them to tell their own story and present the high points of their own civilizations? On reflecting on observations in these areas and trying to see this prospect from a developing country's point of view, the answer is "yes—and no."

The answer is yes when that which can be projected is perceived to be in the image to which the developing country aspires—modern and prestigious by international definition. Filipinos take pride in their new modern and impressive Cultural Center, Kenyans in their Kenyatta Center, the scene for numerous international conferences. Many national airlines do not make a profit on the international routes, but the modern jets bearing the national identification prove something. Certainly, favorable international attention to their accomplished intellectuals, professionals, modern artists, and diplomats is satisfying.

But past experience in "reverse flow" is not all that reassuring. Indonesians might like to be known for modern designs in batik cloth, but what part of the population with an international awareness really wants to be identified in the late twentieth century with the Borabudur ruins, gamelon orchestras, or shadow puppets? How many Filipinos want to identify with the news that the most primitive people alive in the world today have been discovered in Mindanao—the "Gentle Tasaday," to use the title of a book written about them by an *American* author? The modern Peruvian does not spend much time at the local Inca ruin. Much of what makes these areas exotic and interesting to the international tourist is precisely that which many modernizing local citizens would like to forget, even though the artistry is acclaimed and sought by collectors. Who wants to be the object of a collector's attention?

The point here is that for purposes of international exposure, a considerable self-assurance in one's national identity and in having made it in the modern world is needed *before* the modern elites of these countries will promote their "native" accomplishments and exotic culture with genuine pride and enthusiasm. The Mexican evolution in this regard is instructive; it is something of a success story in national psychology as Aztec past, a living revolution, and modern achievement are blended in national identity.

5

THE EDUCATIONAL DIMENSION
IN INTERNATIONAL COMMUNICATION

Academic and scholarly relations in general and the developing world's particular interest in plugging in to it comprise a rather specialized part of the total spectrum of America's international communication processes. American dominance in scholarly affairs and in a one-way flow of educational materials and techniques, as well as of the scholars and educators themselves, does much to shape the total world communication environment. Education, after all, is fundamental to the capacity to communicate on even the most elementary level in the international arena. What goes into the education process determines in large measure the knowledge base and habits of thinking that people will carry into their interaction across national borders. In Chapter 2 we referred to the advantageous position held by the United States by virtue of its increasing function as college professor to the world. Here, beyond the impact on students, we will be concerned first with academic professionals and with their international traffic in educational and scientific fields, and then we will consider several factors and trends in the educational relationship related to technology transfer as observed in the pilot country studies. There is little chance that present patterns will soon be reversed, certainly not with the ongoing drive for access to technology and the trend toward English as its language, also mentioned earlier.

Whether or not one is interested in academic affairs, this dimension needs to be kept in mind if a reliable perspective on U.S. communication is to be gained. Certainly educational relations in one form or another are coming to make up a significant part of the total U.S. international relations process.

THE STATE OF ACADEMIC AND
SCHOLARLY RELATIONSHIPS

The logical starting point is officially sponsored educational and cultural exchange, as in the Fullbright government-sponsored exchange of scholars—from graduate students to more senior postgraduate fellows and even distinguished professionals in scientific and cultural fields. By examining how that program has developed over time, one can note a number of factors that have come to affect the broader field of American academic relationships. It is somewhat easier to follow trends in the case of Fulbright exchange as public policy is involved, priorities are debated, and trends that affect the rationale of the program have more occasion to be considered. Actually, encrusted institutionalization has resisted profound review in the various official and semi-official agencies involved. Yet because the Fulbright program is directed toward *mutual* understanding objectives—vague though that concept is—changing factors become policy problems that demand attention.

When Senator J. William Fulbright first initiated the program that has made his name so well-known around the world, thoughtful educators were most concerned with problems of conflict resolution, causes of war, and measures that might prevent its repetition. It appeared that civilized people, for all their accomplishments, had understood their neighbors so inadequately that a holocaust of the scale of World War II could be set off. With the prospects for future peace dependent on better performance, these leaders were looking for ways to break down the walls of limited comprehension of one society for another, of too little knowledge of other cultures and world views. At the very least, if the intellectual leaders and future elites of the nations that had made war could come to have a better comprehension of the reality of other places, and could establish habits of mutual cooperation, an important resource for gaining a more problem-solving world would be available. If there could be a broad enough circle of such people, their influence might help override misperceptions and the flashpoints of chauvinistic confrontation or wounded honor. Reason might better carry its weight against passion in the international arena. Further, greater appreciation for the accomplishments of other civilizations as seen in their art and literature, philosophy and science, might permit a better understanding of the inner meaning of life in, for example, Germany, Japan, or the United States. In any case, the sharing of such accomplishment could lead to greater enrichment for all.

This was the pattern of concerns from which the Fulbright and related programs were initiated. The context essentially was the industrialized world, the countries which made the difference in the balance of world power, the areas in which future large-scale warfare—now atomic warfare—posed the greatest threat. The emphasis on *mutual* understanding was genuine. The Fulbright program was an investment in peaceful coexistence through broader perspectives and mutual respect.[1]

All this was rather imprecise at the time, and looking back we see that events have changed the sense of priorities to produce more of a one-way exchange. Two major factors stand out for their effect. The first was the ideological standoff of the Cold War, and the sense of deadly competition that went with it for "winning hearts and minds"— persuading, affecting public opinion, advocating beliefs and institutions. This had a direct impact on the implicit logic of educational and cultural exchange programs. *Mutual* understanding was not really the objective; a one-way understanding was more to the point. When Americans went abroad under these programs, they became an exhibition of the American way of life, practitioners of democracy, articulate spokesmen, defenders of the faith. They were there less to develop their understanding of another way of life—indeed, this might even be suspect—than to proselytize. The Fulbrighter had to exercise extreme care in being too coldly objective, especially if such objectivity appeared to give the U.S. a negative image. Security clearances were instituted partly to assure selection of loyal representatives, and partly to avoid the embarrassment that would follow if a recipient of public funds should turn out to be a critic and undermine the Cold War effort. While in reality much of the program did operate in its intended and normal way, there was a public single-mindedness of the times that changed the priorities.

The selection of foreign grantees for travel to the United States was also affected, probably even more so. For these grants represented what was seen as an opportunity to influence foreign intellectual and political leaders, present and future, when they could see America first hand. To see us as we really are is to love us, or so seemed to be the logic. Visitor programs for important foreign leaders were stepped up as a good defense against hostile ideological propaganda. It was believed that the proof could be documented in the results, at least if some selective cases were employed. Record was kept of specific Fulbright and international visitor alumni who became chiefs of state, cabinet ministers, and political leaders. Year after year, well into the 1970s, budget requests for the State Department's Bureau of Educational and Cultural Affairs were justified by a recounting of these successes. The implicit assumption was

[1]For an account of how this worked out in the early years, see Henry J. Kellermann, *Cultural Relations as an Instrument of U.S. Foreign Policy—The Educational Exchange Program between the United States and Germany 1945–1954* (Washington: Department of State Publication 8931, 1978).

that by some mysterious chemistry these visitors would have received a wholesome degree of persuasion that would make a difference. Somehow the record was lost of those grantees who returned with their critical judgments of the United States confirmed, or who went on to become thorns in the flesh of ideological dialogue, their prickliness augmented by the strength of first-hand experience!

In retrospect, a large amount of international education *was* achieved and many misperceptions *were* defused, despite a naive quality in the undertaking. Certainly the American side of the Cold War conflict came off better by this open method than did that of the opponents with their widely known "iron curtain." But the point for the discussion here is that the mutual understanding process came to be understood as a matter of first understanding the United States.

Another related program that gained momentum during this era probably generated suspicion of American meddling intentions. This was the effort championed by Robert Kennedy to "reach youth!" The campaign was promoted as an urgent investment in winning the Cold War. The foreign affairs establishment went to extraordinary lengths to pursue this objective. There were "youth" programs in every Embassy, youth officers, youth plans, youth committees, reporting requirements, budgets, and additions to the Washington bureaucracy. There was a certain problem in defining "youth"—were they the Boy Scouts, students, perhaps middle-aged labor leaders who still might come into prominence and leadership? Some cynics noted that had anyone tried to "reach youth" in the United States he would have had a hard time predicting just who would become influential. They might have missed Harry Truman or Barry Goldwater altogether, for example. Most interesting of all, there was an almost complete absence of any suggestion of just what you would tell youth if you should happen to "reach" them. All the emphasis was on the mechanisms. It was assumed that the message would be self-evident—an innocence of the highest order in cross-cultural communication.

Another factor pushing the Fulbright and other exchange programs into a one-way mode was the emergence of so many new nations, most of them facing heavy tasks in political and economic development. The conception of the program changed in several ways. In the first place, as the total number of countries involved in exchange agreements enlarged greatly, exchange was no longer so predominantly with the larger and more educationally developed countries where a real exchange was credible and had value for both sides. Further, given the Cold War preoccupations already noted, the competition was to win the new members of the international community to the democratic fold. Exchange objectives were amended accordingly.

But the new economic development objective itself also led to an America-centric quality in exchange relationships. Knowledge transfer and technical assistance became a priority concern on both sides, and the number of organizations and programs offering international education and training opportunities increased enormously. The Fulbright program thus became less unique, especially as Fulbright commissions yielded to pressures to use more and more of available grants for what were essentially technical assistance objectives. It was regularly assumed that some mutual understanding would be gained, but actual decisions were increasingly based, for example, on which faculty of a developing university needed an American specialist to build the curriculum, or which fields most needed to have its students in U.S. graduate programs.

This posed a severe dilemma for the rationale of the Fulbright program as all exchange programs with countries in the developing world, and with some others as well, have tended to be perceived as additional resources for technical assistance. And "mutual understanding" is an amorphous objective when it competes with the nuts-and-bolts of technical assistance. Thus, frequently the Fulbright program has been reduced to not only simply another resource, but a minor one at that, given the total increase in grant opportunities. Malaysia is a case in point. For many years the Fulbright program there enjoyed high prestige and competition for the grants was keen. This luster diminished in the 1970s to the great discouragement of the Commission that expended time and effort on the selection process. But note what had happened in the statistics: in 1974, for example, the number of grants available was in the range of five for Americans to come to Malaysia, and six for Malaysians to go to the United States. Against this flow, Malaysia already had a *majority* of its students in higher education studying abroad; while 15,000 were enrolled in the five universities in Malaysia, 26,000 Malaysians were studying abroad, according to Malaysian government statistics. Most of these were in Commonwealth countries, and about 2,000 were in the United States. (Many of the total were ethnically Chinese who, in any case, had difficulty getting into local universities given the preference extended to Malays to help them catch up in this multi-ethnic nation.)

Developmental educational assistance to Malaysia was made available from 57 foreign sources: 26 foreign governments and international organizations, 31 private and semi-governmental organizations. This brought 788 people from abroad to Malaysia to provide training, teaching, or technical counsel (excluding volunteers); 851 Malaysians were

sent abroad. At the same time the Malaysian government itself was supporting foreign education for development purposes. In the case of
Kebangsaan University, a Malay institution with an enrollment of about
2,600, some 200 of its faculty and graduate students were abroad at
Malaysian expense.[2]

Thus, the function served by a dozen American Fulbright grants
had changed markedly over the years. Little unique purpose was served
by 1974. Responsible officials were faced with the problem of defining a
special purpose or of terminating it if the original intentions of the
Fulbright program were to be preserved.

Zambia represents perhaps an extreme example of priority given
to technical assistance and educational development as it was among the
least prepared at independence to supply its own trained and educated
manpower for leadership positions. So American exchange activity has
been heavily development-oriented. By the end of Zambia's first ten
years as a nation, nearly 500 Zambians had received grants for study in
the United States, about half of these being AID grants, the rest those of
various exchange programs including the Fulbright program. But the
American input had become relatively modest. A U.N. survey for 1975
showed that foreign assistance to Zambia came from 25 different countries (21 extending some form of assistance in the education field), 13
multilateral organizations, and a number of private and religious
groups. About 2,350 people were involved in some form of educational
and technical exchange, either coming to Zambia or going abroad for
training. Nine hundred of these were in the educational development
sector itself, with British teachers and professors in Zambia on plans
which "topped off" their salaries making up at least half of that number.
Separate statistics showed that in 1975 about 460 Zambians were studying in British institutions of higher education.

In sum, U.S. government-sponsored exchange programs, and related programs as well, face the problem of rechecking their rationale
for relevance in today's communication environment if mutual understanding is still the goal. The Cold War is over, and new elites are not
easily manipulated anyway. Technical assistance has its own momentum,
and adding a few drops to the stream will have little effect. The one-way
conception that has been generated needs review. An appropriate conception of mutual understanding for an era of interdependence is just
beginning to be formulated. We will speak further about this in the last
chapter.

---

[2]These data are taken from a study undertaken by Dr. Hans H. Indorf in 1975 for
the Malaysian-American Commission on Cultural Exchange, Kuala Lumpur, Malaysia.

Another arena of international scholarly and educational communication that has been salient is "area studies," a field receiving diminishing attention now, but one which has made a heavy impact on international scholarship, and which presents both the benefits and the scars of a preponderant American initiative. The problem here is more a matter of one-way advantage than one-way flow, for most of the area study effort has been designed to meet American intellectual and scientific curiosity and to gain the basic knowledge Americans have needed to carry out the responsibilities they have assumed in world affairs. In fact, much of the impetus for Area Study programs came in the Defense Education Act of 1958, and its Title VI. By this act dozens of area studies centers have been created in American universities and a generation of specialists has been trained in areas from the South Pacific to Western Europe.

Actually, area studies are going through somewhat discouraging times. Increasing difficulties in studying abroad, the changing emphasis in academia (by which the narrower disciplines fare better in the job market than cross-disciplinary area specialization), and reduced financial support have taken their toll. Nevertheless, this is an essential and still vital aspect of communication among educators, and the basis of much scholarly collaboration across national boundaries. Distinguished centers still stand out including Cornell's Southeast Asia Center, Harvard's East Asia Center, Africa Centers at Northwestern and the University of California at Los Angeles, the Latin American Program at the University of Texas, and the University of Chicago's South Asia Center. The last has carried much of the initiative for the American Institute of Indian Studies, a research and activity arm of a number of cooperating universities. Columbia University maintains an international center which covers several areas. These more mature centers have become real crossroads for collaborative research, including participants from the world areas involved. In many cases they have counterpart institutions in the countries where they work.

Several trends affect interaction and communication among these academics and scholars. First is a substantial change in the priorities of the international scholarly community itself since area studies expanded to meet post-war needs in the 1950s and early 1960s. This in part has reduced demand for area study products as such. Some of this reduction has been the consequence of success; much of the basic work to fill in the gaps of knowledge in such fields as history, anthropology, geography, earth sciences, and linguistics has been accomplished. In the process, the areas being studied have gained their own trained specialists able to conduct their own studies.

Further, the kind of knowledge now needed tends to be a more complex analysis of contemporary developments. For this many disciplines have developed a recognizable multinational community of scholars with common analytical approaches. Economics would be one along with such other fields as the physical and biological sciences, medicine, demography, and linguistics. The end result is that "area" approaches in many fields of inquiry are being absorbed into larger world frames of reference by transnational collegiums of scholars whose attention is directed to more general or multi-area problems. That is, for better or worse, the cross-national inquiry has become *subject*-oriented rather than specifically *area*-oriented. Thus, an economist might study entrepreneurship in developing countries rather than undertake a more narrow study of the business culture of India, and would do it as a member of an international community of specialists interested in the phenomenon. The number of disciplines that hold international meetings has increased very substantially over the last 20 years. In this milieu, it is professionally less advantageous for an interdisciplinary group of scholars to organize research that uses a given country or area as a target. They have become too discipline-specific in interest and career application. This helps establish transnational linkages within disciplines, although it may not do much for integrated understanding of cultural areas themselves.

Nationalism and political sensitivity have now increased the barrier to foreign specialists working in many countries. The visas are harder to obtain, and permission for unrestricted research is more reluctantly granted. In most of the countries in the pilot studies, it was apparent that the general public, and even the more remote indigenous communities were becoming, like the American Indians, weary of outsiders coming to study them for the benefit of their foreign intellectual and often patronizing curiosity. It was difficult enough when it was the exotic and unusual that attracted foreign researchers. When foreign scholars directed their attention toward political institutions, fear of invidious comparison and suspicion regarding the use to be made of such research reduced the readiness to cooperate. Images of the CIA, the much-publicized (usually inaccurately) Camelot project in Chile, and the sensational use made of materials by pseudo-researchers have resulted in an uncongenial public opinion.

The stage may be set for better future international collaboration. The reasons for negative reaction to past American style and dominance have been recognized and remedial steps are being taken toward a more collegiate basis for continued work. A lingering problem is that modern scholars in developing academic fields in many countries are chafing at a situation in which much of the basic research on their own countries has been done *for* them by foreign specialists, with the data, and in the case of archaeology even the artifacts, having been taken away for processing somewhere else. Research has typically been published in Europe or America with only a minimum recognition of native collaboration. Thus, these new professionals find that they have to rely on foreign sources for the best information on their own societies, and in many cases, actually go to places like Cornell, Pennsylvania, Harvard, or UCLA to train for specialization in their own home area.

As one of the more obvious examples of problems in area research cooperation, overbearing style has been a reason for lingering resentments in the case of India. During the height of American area study there, the 1960s, from 300 to 500 American students and scholars typically could be found in India at one time. When today one hears charges of "academic imperialism," the reasons seem fairly clear. This onslaught was sweeping up information essentially for American benefit. It supplied material to sustain some 15 area study centers in the United States. Often India was a "case study" because it presented an extraordinarily attractive "laboratory" for comparative study of phenomena in many academic fields, and a testing and proving ground for theory and research methodology. India's sharp contrast with Europe and America in cultures and social arrangements, religion and philosophy, languages, climate, and physical environment provided a resource essential for scientific method—a way to find out whether the hypothesis proves out when so many of the possible variables are changed. Weaknesses in methods of observation or data collection could be revealed when tried out in a totally new human or physical environment. The object has been in many instances to advance the discipline; what was learned about India was merely a fringe benefit. This research for nonIndian objectives has not been easily accepted. Indians have felt that they have been *used* for the benefit of someone else's academic and scholarly success, that what was studied did not match Indian priorities.

Indians felt that, after all, they knew their own society best, and that too often Indian reality was bent to fit the theoretical model. Foreign investigators, scientists though they might have been, were inclined to see what they wanted to see, or were too superficial in their knowledge of India to fit what they observed into the meaning of the system. Further, the Indian specialist has felt that comparative analysis has tended to be disparaging in implication, especially when the most traditional behavior, the most remote tribe, or the least effective bureaucratic organization has been singled out to make the best comparative case.

Indians at many levels of academic and scholarly affairs who worked with little pay or recognition for American researchers—often inexperienced graduate students who were well fed and financed by

Indian standards—have found that their translation services and assistance in gathering data were appreciated but their insight in the analysis was not. The end result is that Indians are determined to gain control over researching their own country. During the 1971–75 period restrictions were especially tight, coinciding with a low point in U.S.–Indian relations in general. American research in India had nearly stopped.

Singapore presents another instance of determination to gain control. The Institute for Southeast Asian Studies there has found it politically wise to become established first as a legitimate center for Southeast Asian scholars. It now accepts Americans as fellows in limited numbers, but with insistence that the subjects of research be those consistent with its own on-going research interests, and that results be published in Singapore.

All this is resulting in new and healthier trends. Americans are setting new guidelines. High on the list are requirements that arrangements be made for genuinely collaborative research programs and sponsorship by institutions in the area being studied. Still, some subjects tend to be held out-of-bounds for outsiders. Typically these are political institutions and processes, social integration and change, studies of the primitive and exotic, and studies which tend to document backwardness as seen by modern standards.

THE THIRD WORLD'S VESTED INTEREST IN PLUGGING IN TO AMERICAN KNOWLEDGE AND TECHNOLOGY

America's future role in a global society will depend to an important extent on the quality of its communication relationships with what is now called the Third World. The patterns are now being set in several rather clearly defined channels, one of which is the interaction related to technology transfer. Terms like "First World and "Third World" are too facile, of course; perhaps the "north–south" designation is more correctly descriptive. But however defined, and without trying to draw the demarcation lines too precisely, a number of newer and developing countries do have a vested interest in communicating with the developed Western world. By way of their channels of communication they want access to the knowledge and technology resources that must be tapped if they are to take a place in modern living. For most this means at least a number of trips to the American storehouse. Even the "Second World" has to do this occasionally, from the People's Republic of China to the Soviet Union. This circumstance is not likely to change very soon, but whether it does or not, the habits of cooperation set now are likely to persist.

To recapitulate a bit, we have said that the West's view of what the Third World has to gain by Western association is not always the same as the Third World's view. Most particularly, modernization is not necessarily seen as trying to duplicate the governmental and social arrangements of the United States—or of other Western nations or the Soviet Union, for that matter. Nor is it seen as adopting forms of institutions or copying models that have possibly worked well in other social and cultural soil. Increasingly, Third World leaders feel that reality will force them to evolve the forms that are appropriate for their own societies. Thus, while they have a continuing vested interest in knowing what the Western experience is, this interest is not the compulsion to choose between one system or another.

But we have also said that Third World leaders and elites do want access to the knowledge and technology which sustains modernization. They want to be plugged in to the source, which they see as essentially the United States via the English language, the more so where specialized knowledge and technology are concerned. And they want this access while retaining control of the process; they want advice and counsel without prescription and tutelage. The trend is that as more and more of the basic knowledge is gained by their own professional specialists and spread around in their own university programs, the demand for foreign resources turns to the more highly technical and specialized content and to new and current innovations and applications. We noted that the Fulbright program, for instance, has yielded to this motivation to a large degree.

While the developing countries want and need to maintain a close knowledge transfer relationship with the United States, there are, however, certain problem areas as seen from their point of view which affect the course of cooperation and the quality of the relationship. Several of these will be singled out for discussion here.

INSIDE THE DEVELOPING WORLD LOOKING OUT

Most analyses of the development process tend to look at the less developed areas as a doctor looks at his patients. It is the view from the outside looking in to prescribe where manipulation and treatment is needed here and there to place the patient on the road to health. From the *inside* the pains and the constraints on treatment look different. This affects the dialogue; it explains why people on the two sides talk past each other regarding the path to modern performance. As national leadership elites come to recognize fully that their nation's eventual development will really depend on their own planning genius and managerial capacity, not on foreign advisors and their development plans, a first priority tends to go to increasing the size and capability of the local elite itself. This often tacit reasoning was well-advanced in the countries of the pilot studies, and by all accounts seems evident in many other countries, including those which have chosen the communist route.

The problem for these modernizing leaders, once they recognize the limitations of foreign advisors, is where to start in their national development. It is here that their view from the inside diverges substantially from that of their more optimistic, if unrealistic, Western assistance advisors who impersonally think in terms of the way the total national system works, or who idealistically focus on the "poorest of the poor." The inside view is less optimistic. For example, the sheer magnitude of the task of bringing their rural poor into the mainstream of modern economic life is overwhelming and discouraging. Consider the vast sea of humanity in rural Egypt or Indonesia, India or Pakistan. Leaders and elites sense the inertia of tradition, ignorance and provincial suspicion in ways the foreign advisor is not likely to see except in the abstract. They sense the strain on their own capabilities, resources, and steadfastness of purpose. They have already experienced the political fragility that goes with rapid social change, with Iran a dramatic and current example. And they know their personal appetites and impatience for enjoying modern life.

It is understandable, then, that at least in the short-run more enthusiastic attention is directed toward developing the modern and urban sectors and the emerging middle class. Leaders plan bravely for full national development, but with a certain fatalistic realization that the poor they always have with them. Or they rationalize that the problems of the rural mass will not be met until the more modern part of the society has developed the competence and resources to take on a national task of the proportions posed by their peasant populations. In their view, modern city apartment houses, city parks, technological institutes, and sophisticated equipment for the military are not misplaced priorities. They do not feel that being all poor together is the best way to edge into the 21st century, unless one is to accept the discipline and dedication—and regimentation—of the Communist ideologists.

The end result is even more pressure to tap into the knowledge and technological base of the West. Both the desire to speed their own urban, industrializing middle class development and their need to achieve the competence necessary to take on the truly gigantic task of total national development add to the pressure to get the knowledge and skills to increase effective performance in the central government, in its ministries, in the military, and in the modern industrial and commercial sectors of the society.

Developing self-assurance is also a necessary part of the task. The foreign advisor has this himself, especially the American whose culture reflects a "can-do" set of assumptions about planning and executing. The American people have conquered the frontier, have won wars, and gained world prominence. This self-assurance is dented only by troubles like the Viet Nam experience and the increasing problem of dealing with an ambiguous and interdependent world in which Americans do not control all the factors. Still the advisor is optimistic, and tends not to doubt that even the biggest problems can be solved. The one option not considered is to do nothing.

Take Egyptian or Shah-era Iranian self-assurance as midstream examples. Their outlook has been more complicated than that of Americans as they looked to their national responsibilities. In both cases their elites have wanted to achieve a satisfying national identity for which recognized performance in the modern world is important. Both have suffered from the more generalized image of Middle Eastern backwardness, from which they have tried to divorce themselves. Both have looked back with pride to a long history of high civilization and eminence in their part of the world. But their real circumstances today present a painful contradiction. These two peoples of ancient prestige, who discovered mathematics and established empires, are dependent upon much newer Western countries to gain the basic knowledge and technology needed to emerge into a modern world out of what is seen as a rather static society. And they have not conquered any frontiers in modern history; rather they have been trampled almost at the will of the greater powers. To add to the indignity, the U.S. ethnocentrically has sent its Peace Corps—its children by Middle East standards—to help them solve their problems! (This ended in a psychological stand-off in Iran well before the Shah's departure.)

All this makes it harder to be self-assured in facing profoundly difficult development problems, and it increases sensitivity in working with foreign advisors. Thus psychologically conditioned, evidence of success and new stature assume particular importance in communication relations. Iran's ability under the Shah to plan ahead with their own financial resources, hire foreign specialists, and assume near-great power status changed their stance with outsiders. At best it was a sense of confident equality: at worst, an indulged arrogance. The percentage of the 40,000 American technicians, consultants, and their families in Iran at the time who were happy in their relationships with their Iranian counterparts was extraordinarily low. As became evident when the curtain was pulled aside by the downfall of the Shah, the complicated relationship with Americans was partly a matter of poor cross-cultural communication, and partly a function of tension among Iranians themselves under a regime of force-fed social change. During interviews there, a thoughtful Iranian observed that some of the apparent resentment toward Americans at that time was basically resentment of nonEnglish-speaking Iranians toward their English-speaking fellow citizens who benefited from the American association and the programs being carried out by the Shah.

This concern with modern performance also helps explain the enormous Egyptian satisfaction when their military forces *did* perform on an acceptable *modern* standard in the 1973 war with Israel. A teacher in Alexandria reported in 1976, three years after the event, that when school children were given time for free expression in their art classes, they still depicted the recrossing of the Suez canal over and over again.

The symbolic importance of successful ventures in modern performance is seen in many places. The steel mill and petrochemical plant, Brazilian architecture, the luxury hotel, the sports stadium, the superhighway all have psychological importance as a kind of therapy in self-assurance. And again, it explains the rush to Western resources often for the most technologically sophisticated training and materials—sometimes seen as a misdirection of priorities by Western advisors.

In this context, the American assistance philosophy of extending assistance to the poorest segments of recipient countries runs into impediments. There is considerable reason to predict that this quest will fall far short of expectations, and like the miscast Alliance for Progress in Latin America, will be judged as the naive attempt of Americans to produce consequences in areas in which the social and decision-making factors have been poorly understood. The day is past, it can be argued, when outside assistance institutions will have the leverage to bypass the new elites and their priorities to "reach" the dependent lower segments of the social structures of these countries. In the longer perspective, it will be the local leadership itself that will make the decisions and take the actions that will determine the modernization of their traditional masses, not the outside manipulator. So the current fad in development, to "reach the poorest of the poor," would seem to be a sociological and political nonstarter. Already the more experienced development assistance specialists are rather desperately looking for ways to get around this mandate so that they can carry on in programs which can work through existing Third World planning elites and still somehow be called "reaching the poorest."

THE MANAGEMENT CRISIS

There is now a new problem dimension in modernization that adds incentive to seek knowledge transfer from the United States. This concerns the management field. It is one thing to gain specific skills in, for example, soil chemistry, accounting, medicine, industrial manufacture. It is another to make all the skills and procedures fit together in modern functioning institutions.

This is especially the area in which frustration is building. The shortfall in performance is in coordinating what people do so that the sum is larger than the parts, in scheduling programs in rational sequence, in anticipating contingencies, and in making what one government ministry or one industry does fit into overall patterns. In short, the problem is to make the many parts of the system work together.

Hence, there is a rapidly expanding interest in management, with the belief that Americans are the best managers and that they can supply the best management training. In fact, one of the major fringe benefits derived from the many American corporations that have operated in developing countries is the supply of managerial skill they have left behind. Their higher-level local employee "graduates" have played key and vital roles in country after country where the lack of management resources has placed a premium on their availability. Much of the current need is business management, of course. But it goes well beyond that. At the government level, it means allocation of resources, accomplishing national purpose by orchestrating the energies of a wide variety of institutions that are crucial to national performance. Basically, it is the ability to make complex organizations work. In colonial or imperialist days this dimension was provided from outside; now it has to be accomplished from within.

Africa presents a special context for the demand for management skills. A central motivation is the desire to replace expatriate managers with their own citizens. After 15–18 years of independence, the pressure to run one's own affairs with one's own people is mounting; politically the situation is becoming more sensitive as the lack of this skill dimension becomes more apparent.

Necessarily, large numbers of European and other expatriates have been retained to fill the technical and managerial positions that make modern enterprises operate. When trains run on time, aircraft are maintained, factories produce smoothly, government budgets are reliable, a ministry's plans are technically workable, the chance is high that an Englishman or a Frenchman is unobtrusively carrying on. In 1976, as much as 75% of the faculty of the University of Zambia were expatriates,

95

as were some entire faculties in the University of Nairobi. Kenya has maintained a certain expatriate infrastructure as national policy; the Ivory Coast leans on expatriates, mostly French, without apology to achieve the high pace of development that so impresses the visitor there. Zambia has tried to replace them faster—some critics say too fast. Cameroon has tried harder than the Ivory Coast to make the transition from French to native executives.

White expatriates are not especially resented personally, in fact they are often highly respected. But the need to rely on them *is* resented. And it would be nice to have the salaries going to the home team. Part of the expatriates are African from neighboring countries, for example, well-trained black South Africans, Nigerians (Ibos, typically), and Ugandan exiles. Interestingly, they tend to be more resented, particularly when they signal an air of superiority toward their hosts. Asians, especially in East Africa, provide many of the skills for commerce (profiting accordingly), and also fill many teaching and technical positions. They are most resented of all. Whatever the negative feeling was in Kenya during the regime of Uganda's Idi Amin, Kenyans did not fault him very much for expelling the Asians.

The drive, then, is to be able to replace these people with competent local nationals, or at least reasonably competent. Again, it is increasingly recognized that there is a special skill needed, that of making complex organizations work, of fitting the parts of a system together, the need to know how to manage and administrate. This is the real crisis for self-government, and the real difficulty in replacing expatriates.

The frustration which results when otherwise technically competent people are prematurely placed in managerial roles was widely commented upon in all three African countries in the pilot study. Apart from the obvious difficulties for the enterprises involved, apparently there is a high incidence of personality breakdown under the pressure and inability to cope, to make objective decisions about people, to plan for contingencies. Symptoms run a wide range: withdrawal, paranoid authoritarianism, alcoholism.

Thus, management training becomes a growth industry throughout the Third World. The Harvard Business School was active in the Shah's Iran where the most renowned could be afforded; AID sponsored seminars in business training in Cameroon. A wide variety of enterprising management consulting firms are going overseas.

Egypt has been especially hard-pressed. The lack of coordination by government decision-makers, along with the internal inconsistencies and overlapping of government bureaucracy, had reached spectacular levels and appeared to be a principal impediment in attracting the kind of foreign investment which Egypt's new open door economic policy of the mid-1970s envisioned. The new openness came at a time when many enterprises with headquarters in Beirut were looking for a new Middle East location because of the Lebanese war. But Egypt had difficulty rising to the managerial performance needed to reassure the investor. Egypt too turned to the Americans. For instance, a first seminar in management offered by the American University in Cairo admitted 37 people, 21 of whom were at least of Deputy Minister rank in the government.

Unfortunately, management training is probably seen as more of a magic formula than is realistic. The extraordinary interest in it, and the preference to turn to the U.S. to get it on the assumption that this is where success is proven, give some reason for concern. The two sides of the coin look something like this:

Seen positively, this is a particularly propitious area for American communication in an increasingly interdependent world. As one looks ahead, it is precisely the managers of complex organizations of all kinds—the directors of government agencies, managers of volunteer organizations, university administrators, and those in all phases of economic and financial activity—who will be doing much of the significant international communicating and problem solving. Thus, their ability to do this on the same wave length, and with a congenial mesh with American patterns, is obviously significant. Also, the Third World managerial group will have increasing need, in its own interest, to gain the kind of international and inter-dependence perspective that can be produced in international managerial training and development activities. Pragmatically, they need, and Americans need for them to have a greater understanding of the American scene and the style of decision-making and execution that goes with it. For it is not likely that the United States will suddenly fail to occupy the center of gravity in managing all kinds of internationally significant institutions, from multinational corporations to the Red Cross.

The importance of being able to mesh managerial styles has been demonstrated in American–Japanese relations, a case in which considerable attention has been given to the factors involved. Cross-cultural differences have been pronounced; they could hardly be ignored if essential cooperation was to be achieved. And accommodation is being reached. For instance, Japanese who have set up factories in the United States have made changes in their expectations as to how to relate to their American managerial officers—even though the employees still have to learn to sing the company song in the morning. And Americans try to enhance their negotiating skills by reading a book written in English for their benefit by an internationally sophisticated Japanese writer entitled *Never Take Yes for an Answer* (Imai, 1975)!

One can expect that in the future there will be many occasions for managers of all nations and in both the public and private sectors to be able to communicate even outside their special fields of primary responsibilities. Many new cross-national problems will require their dialogue, such as those at the interface of science and technology with society and environment, or the moral and ethical aspects of managing toward alternative societal objectives. They will face public interest concerns, as many groups in many places perceive management as simply a more efficient way to manipulate or exploit, or in some cases to serve the ends of the larger multinational businesses. In sum, managers will become as important in global society as they are in the more advanced industrial nations already, and their ability to interact with minimum misperception and misunderstanding is in everyone's interest.

On the other hand, however, transferring management skills from the United States probably will not be as easily accomplished as in the case of other skills. Some degree of frustration can be anticipated as superficial formal training exercises do not produce the hoped-for wonders. Much of what makes modern management practice work as it does in the United States is not simply the teachable substance of procedures and organization charts or the techniques of delegating responsibility, but also the less teachable implicit assumptions which are rooted in the cultural base and which remain largely out of the explicit awareness of Western management specialists. These include cause-and-effect reasoning, abstract conceptions of contingency factors, achievement motivation, and a broad general understanding of the many technical and special processes which go into complex undertakings. There is simply the manager's experience of being socialized in a society where the management mentality is accepted as a matter of course, where even the Parents and Teachers Association committee chairman says, "Let's get this thing organized!" There are many subtle role expectations that go with effective management and an activism not always appreciated by people for whom the management function is still new. It has been noted that Kenyans returning from their visits to the United States report their surprise in finding how hard important people work—a contradiction in terms to the Kenyan elite pattern of expectations.

PLUGGING IN TO THE U.S.
EDUCATION INDUSTRY

Knowledge and technology transfer comes in many forms, from technical journals, the service manuals that come with Western equipment, working in an industry in the West, even via returning illegal immigrants. But the most direct access is by tapping into the extremely broad and varied Western educational industry, an industry that can supply both basic and applied courses, and cover a range of subjects from hotel management to atomic physics. This is not as straightforward a process as might be assumed, especially as seen from the Third World experience. Besides cost and logistics, there are significant cultural and institutional gaps to bridge.

This transfer process is largely a matter of *coming* to the U.S., and this the developing world does. Their students make up a large part of the 250,000 foreign students currently in the United States. They come as individuals; they get scholarships from the U.S. Government and host institutions, foreign universities send them to develop their own faculties. They come for advanced medical training and hospital experience. Religious groups sponsor foreign students. Specialists come on a vast array of bilateral and multilateral technical and economic development programs, and private companies and businesses send employees for special training. About 75,000 such specialist visitors enter the U.S. each year.

Especially in recent years, they come on programs initiated and financed by their own governments as investments in the development process, sometimes including very pinpointed projects such as preparation for diplomatic service or military command. The Egyptian Missions program, discussed earlier, is an example of one of the older programs; it was started in the 1920s. The high volume traffic today, comes, however, from countries where new income from higher petroleum prices has suddenly provided the means to invest heavily in the knowledge transfer process. Venezuela favors its young people from the more educationally disadvantaged provincial areas for technical study abroad. Most of them are coming to the United States; the Venezuelan government has set up its own facilities in the United States just to place and administer the student flow. Under the Shah, Iran officially sponsored thousands of students despite their political activism once abroad. Nigeria has increasing numbers, and the Middle East petroleum producers send their people with almost frenetic urgency. The Saudi Arabian elite typically go to the University of Southern California. One of the main missions of the cultural attaché offices in foreign embassies in Washington is to attend to their training programs in the United States. One of the largest American institutions dedicated to foreign educational programming is the Institute of International Education in New York. The American Friends of the Middle East, and the African–American Institute supply services for their areas.

The first task is selecting institution and program. Typically, visitors come with fixed ideas about prestige universities—namely, those they have heard about, and which their colleagues back home will have heard about. The Harvard, MIT, University of California, Michigan State syndrome has to be overcome for most aspirants in favor of entering some less internationally renowned university or special school that most probably has the more appropriate program. The potential student also has to be wary of over-eager recruiting on the part of institutions hard pressed to maintain enrollment in difficult financial times. The enthusiasm to attract foreign students may not match facilities for offering the programs they need.

But with these matters resolved, important cross-cultural educational problems remain to be surmounted both in the interest of the knowledge transfer process and the quality of international relations in general. Unhappily, in most cases both the foreign visitors and their hosts find themselves on their own in meeting them. Most of the usual and repeated difficulties receive little concerted attention from educational administrators.

The first set of difficulties besets the transition from foreign educational systems to the American, a system which is unique in many aspects ranging from educational philosophy to the social structure of the universities themselves. Generally, the hurdle that attracts most attention, and therefore supporting assistance, is language. But once that problem is eased, there are a host of other adjustment tasks to be accomplished. This those who staff the foreign student advisors offices around the country know only too well, even if they do not always know what to do about them. Some are relatively simple, but difficult none the less— budgeting for American costs, dealing with landlords, understanding the "culture" of the library system, in some cases coping with living routines without servants. The harder problems are those that are not so obvious. If, for example, one comes from Latin America to study law or some field related to it, he will confront the case study method—a bit of legal philosophy and intellectual approach that is new and not easily learnable just by doing the course work. American education uses much more of the inductive approach rather than the deductive that is standard elsewhere. One of the largest problems comes in making a transition from a rote memory or a listen, take notes, play back on examinations approach common in many Third World educational systems, to the emphasis on individual creativity common in the U.S. The American system is one in which students question and perhaps disagree with the professor in the class, and one in which essay questions in the examination call for applying material in problem-solving ways. Even the routine heavy use of books and research material is a new educational experience for those coming from areas where textbooks, and certainly supplemental texts, are scarce. More than is usually realized, independent research is a culturally-conditioned way to engage one's thinking in substantive materials. Even using a university's extracurricular opportunities is something to be learned.

Social relations in a university area present further cross-cultural challenges, sometimes made easier by previous exposure or by the presence of a supportive ethnic community close by. There are large numbers of resident Indians in New York and Chicago, for example. The logic of American casual friendships is different than that in more traditional societies; men–women relations can pose entirely new patterns of role expectations and values. Relating to professors and university staffs in an egalitarian society can often post subtle difficulties for the visitor and for his hosts. The Indian case again: in the universities it is reported that the Indian who is seen as friendly and warm to a colleague, or even deferential to a superior on the organization chart, can appear overbearing and insensitively rude to lesser members of the office staff. Even when he is deferential to superiors, overly-deferential behavior or what is interpreted as obsequiousness, can set off negative reactions in Americans. Adjustment to American-style egalitarianism does not come easily, and it is precisely in this area that Americans can be quickly and emotionally offended. As a tentative explanation, such offending behavior may reflect the logic of social relations in Indian society—always someone to cater to above, and someone to defer to you from below. It starts in family relationships and extends through occupation and public association. While Indians themselves often value their escape from that system to the open American society, social habits are deeply implanted and tend to persist and be manifested out of awareness.

These problems are not easily addressed. Unlike the command of English, they do not affect the local university system clearly enough to demand that something be done. For all the number of foreign students in the U.S., they make up but a tiny proportion of the total student bodies in most academic institutions. Few professors and few departments have the experience or the extra time and energy to adapt what they offer to the special needs of foreign students, who in any case come from so many different cultures and areas that no single remedy would apply. Hence, this aspect of cross-cultural communication is remarkably little-appreciated in the universities—precisely the places where there would seem to be the greatest capacity to comprehend the problem. There are exceptions. Carefully worked-out orientation programs and continuing guidance through the cultural adjustment process, such as the approach taken at the University of Minnesota, have demonstrated that the nettle can be grasped. The National Association of Foreign Student Affairs is one of the principal organizations addressing itself to these matters.

It should be noted that one can easily assume that the cultural adjustment problem is essentially one at the undergraduate level. Actually, much of the use made of universities by foreign educational visitors is at the graduate, and increasingly at the post-graduate level. As a case in point, at the University of Pennsylvania in 1977 there were 76 Indian students enrolled in regular programs in various departments, but there were 46 more "nonstudents" working in more independent specialized advanced projects. These were typically in such fields as medical and physical sciences, mathematics, engineering, and management. This is duplicated repeatedly by other nationalities in many other centers that have advanced laboratories and are conducting research into new and specialized fields.

However, even after having made peace with the American educational culture, another kind of adaptation problem remains. That is making the knowledge and technology gained in the United States transferable to the reality of the developing country and to the needs of the recipient's career environment. The first frequently encountered difficulty is that U.S. education and specialized technological training are packaged for the American market—that is, educational institutions are organized on the assumption that their clients will pursue careers in the United States. In many fields this assumes that a person will need specialized skills, and that he will work in institutions where he is surrounded by other highly specialized people, typically on team endeavors, supported with modern equipment. It therefore teaches the trainee to think of himself as a specialist and to identify with First World standards for the profession in question. All this may turn out to be partly dysfunctional back in the home country. The complaint of sponsors in developing countries is that those who have tried to plug into Western expertise return wanting to do jobs that are more sophisticated than needed or appropriate. They demand laboratory equipment and try to remain in their narrow specialities. When the returnee has no well-equipped laboratory, no computer, no assistants, insufficient hospital equipment, or no supporting colleagues, he has a new adaptation task. Success in this transition varies greatly. In Indonesia, where this aspect of technical assistance has been taken seriously by both the Indonesians and the Americans who have guided much of the U.S. educational effort, results have been reasonably satisfactory. Other programs have been less successful in the adapting process.

The first consideration, if the knowledge and technology transfer is to prosper, is to be sure that the trainee actually returns home. The U.S. educational process understandably tempts the trainee to stay on to apply his new skills in the U.S., the place for which they were designed and where prospects for adequate compensation and standards of living are good. Even when wages and position back home are assured, life in a developing country may have become unattractive in comparison, and the career there appears sure to be frustrating. When income and job prospects are less attractive, as in Egypt or the Philippines, the incentive to remain or to go on to third countries is high. We noted earlier that the Egyptian government complained that of the 2,000 people they have sent largely at their own expense to the United States over the years of its Missions programs, as many as 600 have never returned. Thus, in this brain drain process they feel that they have been subsidizing the United States.

Again, surprisingly little has been done to facilitate adaptation to end user needs. Except when it is part of a purposeful U.S.-sponsored technical assistance program, the burden falls on the Third World individual or institution. Some have enjoyed greater returns from their effort and resources by choosing their candidates for training carefully; generally the more mature person, and the one already more integrated into his home country career system fares best. Sending people in teams has been productive, as has the predeparture orientation and support of colleagues who have been through similar programs. On the American side much could be done by providing flexibility in prescribed courses of study, more imaginative counselling, and by creating curricula designed to fit the needs of foreign clients. Some institutions have done this, especially when they have undertaken contracts to link up with particular overseas institutions or projects, as, for example, Michigan State or the University of Kentucky. The University of California at Los Angeles has tried some innovative programs, spurred by the fact that at times they may have as many as 5,000 foreign students on campus. As falling enrollment in a number of American colleges is making the foreign student more attractive, the incentive to offer specially tailored educational packages is increased accordingly.

There is a further aspect of the adaptation problem that is even less actively taken into account. This arises when the purpose of the foreign specialist is to teach his subject material after he returns to his own country. Thus, some complain that while they received all the benefits of efficient courses and programs, they had no opportunity to learn how their educational programs were produced and delivered, and therefore how they could go about organizing their own courses for local benefit. For instance, if science is the field, one needs to know what goes into planning a laboratory, ordering equipment, designing experiments, and determining standards for student performance. Generally, this attention to the education process itself is formally presented only in departments of education, not in those of physics or business administration. Foreign graduate students are less likely to have had the opportunity to be graduatec assistants, the experience which introduces their American colleagues to educational methodology.

Finally, there is a further approach for plugging into the benefits of the American way of educating. That is to go beyond the subject material and adopt aspects of the U.S. educational system itself. There are transition problems here, too. In the 1960s the Central University of Quito, Ecuador, joined in a plan with American advisors to completely transform the University into an American-style institution. The planning went from standards for a full-time faculty in appropriate academic departments to accounting and supply procedures. Like trying to transplant other institutions into a foreign cultural milieu, this did not work very well, despite the efforts of the American university that was contracted to oversee the process. With a sudden change in government, the project folded. Still, the American Universities operated by Americans in Beirut and Cairo have been highly significant in their impact on modernizing students throughout the Middle East. Their method and approach accomplished something that could not have been duplicated in the area.

However transplantable the American system, much of the developing world is faced with the urgent need to make major changes in their present educational systems in order to bring them into consistency with current circumstances and with modernization aspirations. Their original traditional systems clearly are out of functional compatibility with a world of factories and television programs. And many of the systems which were transplants to begin with—French and British models—also serve current needs poorly, especially as many features of these systems as they were administered in colonial days are retained in institutionalized cement. Educators in East Africa note that the educational system they inherited from the British contrives to train a good supply of clerks and a few candidates for the university, but very few who can fill the technical positions of a modern society. Those who are unable to obtain one of the limited places at the university are not otherwise trained to get jobs after their broad, rather classical education that prepared them for the university entrance examinations. In many cases they still study Greek and Western history, world geography, Western literature (even Beowulf), and formal mathematics. The result is that the country needs trained people that are unavailable, and at the same time young people are not qualified for jobs. Both the English and the French systems have tended to educate people to *be* something rather than to *do* something. The American visitor's attention is repeatedly attracted to the extraordinary sacrifice made in these areas by modern families as they try to send their children to choice schools that will prepare them for qualifying examinations. Thus, they can compete for the "correct" higher education—so they can again pass still further qualifying examinations to be approved for the desirable positions in government and other institutions that require the status degrees. The pressure on students to prepare for these examinations is enormous, and the whole family suffers a traumatic ordeal. Even after final graduation the system is faulted, for then it allows the graduate to stop the learning process. Having been stamped as a graduate he has gained the desired status and there is no further need to learn.

Therefore, there is pressure to change, and to look for alternative approaches. In this context the American education system, despite its domestic problems of "getting back to basics," commands interest in its vocational training in high school and even before, in practical subjects related to local community problems, in junior colleges, even in a different orientation to the learning process and its application. At the university level there is growing appreciation for independent initiative in the search for knowledge, education for action, cumulative semester credit systems rather than final general qualifying exams. In some cases where university instruction is being switched to English, it is suggested that the idea may be as much to switch from old systems and approaches to an American style of learning as it is to use the resources available in the English language.

The temptation is strong both on the part of American advisors and recipients to look for dramatic results by adopting American forms and systems. As in the case of management training, it is difficult to duplicate in another country the many ways in which the American cultural base functions to sustain the educational system within American society so that it produces the results that the system does for Americans. This supporting foundation of assumptions, values, and patterns of thinking cannot be adopted as easily as the institutional forms, so the magic probably will not be produced by a rush to adopt the American formula. Still, the American system is much more consistent in its approach with the modern institutions and performance that are being sought, so the Third World has a compelling reason to maintain a close relationship with American educators and their way of educating.

6

COPING WITH IMAGES
AND MISPERCEPTIONS

If, as we argue, so much will depend on communication in a more global society, then coping with the distorted images and misperceptions which beset the communication process should be a matter of major concern. The issues to be resolved in a tightly knit world will be difficult enough even if communication about them is straightforward and dependably accurate. If the dialogue is confused by mismatched meanings, attempts at problem-solving will get nowhere. This is simply the basic psychology of communication, to be sure, and it applies even at home as in arguing across the generation gap about the use of the family car, or across vested interests in deciding where to locate a new city park. Technically, myths and misperceptions *per se* need not block communication; if people hold the same ones, they can get along. It is when people have different ones that there is trouble. And when the dialogue is international and cross-cultural, there will almost certainly be a problem, whether it be at the person-to-person, public-to-public, or government-to-government level. In this chapter we will emphasize factors in the public's preparation for international communication. The government level will be taken up in Chapter 7.

Actually, the miracle of modern travel and communication technology is that so many people are able to have reasonably accurate mental pictures of other parts of the world. The achievement over the last half century is remarkable; by now, most nations can enjoy the resources of a circle of well-informed and internationally knowledgeable citizens. But increasingly, the way that nations interact is a function of the way that larger publics perceive and reason about issues and events. Hence, it is not necessarily what actually happened or what the facts of the case may be, but what the public *thinks* the facts are that determine the course of relationships. Surveys continually bring up the shocking evidence that even in the United States, the most advanced information society with its universal educational system and media penetration, the image and knowledge base for facing international issues is far from adequate. An example: even in the continuing Middle East conflict, one half of a representative group of high school seniors could not identify Egypt as an Arab country in a simple multiple choice test.[1] Too frequently public leaders in the Congress, government executives, politically appointed ambassadors, and presidents themselves—the people who are called upon to make the most important decisions regarding foreign affairs— assume their duties with no foreign experience, or the most superficial exposure outside the borders of the United States, with limited educational background in international subjects and no knowledge of a foreign language. The same is true in the business world. This makes "coping with images and misperceptions" a very uphill task.

The idea that the images of other societies that we carry in our heads will have something to do with the way we process any new information about them has been around for a long time. One early reminder was Harold Isaacs' descriptive title, *Scratches on Our Minds,* written in 1958. It might be assumed that once aware of these impediments to accurate perception, the intelligent person could take charge of his reasoning processes and override his previous impressions. Psychologists warn us that it is not that easy. A person's perception habits are much more locked in, much more rigidly preprogrammed than one realizes. The problem is that one does not simply perceive afresh on the basis of the sensory impulses that reach the brain. Most especially when the subject is abstract, the item to be perceived is not likely to be seen or heard in its entirety but through partial or symbolic stimuli—the rest of the conception is added from the idea banks of the mind. Humans perceive by bringing to bear the framework of past experience, knowledge, and habitual ways of fitting given cues into a meaningful existing set of understandings and previous ways of processing similar cues and triggering stimuli.

This point deserves emphasis. Even in the most simple perception task, previous experience adds meaning to the actual sensory information. For example, when one "sees" a door, window, or table-top, a judgment can be made quickly that these are rectangular objects even

---

[1]Reported by educational specialists in California. Of course, technically the multiple choice question should have said "Arabic-speaking."

though it is unlikely that the observation is made from such a perfect position that the image on the retina of the eye is in fact a rectangle. But with experience with doors and tables, something is added to the actual stimuli to allow a conclusion. The problem is that this previous experience will be added even though the object is not actually square or rectangular. In modern society the expectation of right angles is so imprinted that it becomes almost impossible to see a variation when it exists. This is the basis for the optical illusions by which the psychological experimenter is able to engage in fun and games with distorted rooms and line drawings.[2]

In the case of social perception or dealing with abstractions, a still larger portion of the contextual information is supplied from memory and previous knowledge, and it is even more difficult to perceive according to some standard of accuracy, or even in the same way as another person. Consider the perceptual processing which must go on when the stimulus is a political statement, a threatening gesture, a cartoon, or the sound of a strange accent. As there is vast research on this, including a growing literature related to international communication, there is no need to pursue the analysis here. The point is that it is very difficult, even with the best of will and determination, to override one's built-in habits of perceiving and reasoning. It is this process of *assigning* meaning to the event or the message that causes concern for international communication, for by being international and usually cross-cultural, it is unlikely that experience will allow one to assign either a fully accurate or objective meaning and significance to a given transmission, or to match the subjective meaning that would be assigned in the context of another culture or national experience. However, the greater the international experience brought to bear, the more dependable the data banks of the mind are likely to be when meaning is assigned to the new event or bit of information.

There is another way to say much the same thing, a way that applies especially well to international relations and particularly to negotiation. This is the idea that, consciously or not, one will attribute *motives* for what the other person does or says. If the situation is ambiguous, some effort may be required, but if the other person is well known, or fits neatly into one's own culture, the chances of accurately attributing motive are high. We "read in" a frame of reference or motive that makes the message or behavior seem consistent and fit into a pattern of our own experience. However, if the other actor is from another culture, or is speaking for a foreign organization or government, the chance of *misattribution* of mo-

[2]The late Hadley Cantril conducted some of the best known experiments in this regard at his laboratory at Princeton, N.J. to demonstrate how difficult it is to override perception habits.

tive is one of the international community's most severe impediments to problem solving. It causes trouble from bargaining in an open market to compiling intelligence estimates for the National Security Council.

The plain fact is that most people are not prepared to conduct international business. They lack not only the necessary understanding of the processes discussed above, but also an appreciation of how subtly difficult cross-cultural communication is and an awareness of how much cultural baggage they carry with them in their own perceptions habits when making evaluations and judgments in even the most routine situations. The mental patterns of one's own group become unquestioned "common sense," and "human nature." This is very functional at home; it plays havoc abroad.

For nations like the United States, with a relatively high degree of public participation in national decision-making, public images and perceptions assume particularly far-reaching significance. Even if responsible government officials are prepared to opt for the international action that best squares with the most accurate perception of the issue at hand, they are constrained, supported, or urged toward other options by the public's sense of the situation. The recent debate over the Panama Canal treaties was a case in point. It was both a difficult test of statesmanship in meeting an international reality to which the American public assigned such varied and emotionally-laden meanings, and a controversial exercise in determining how far a government could go in the international education of its citizens.

A CASE IN POINT; IMAGES AND AMERICAN RELATIONSHIPS WITH INDIA

The course of American relationships with modern India is illustrative of the problems that images present in public-to-public communication. Many of the points to be made will apply elsewhere, especially as Americans will actually interact and conduct their business mostly with more urban, industrialized, and educated sectors of the developing world as in the case of India.

One of the main factors complicating dialogue with Indians involves conflicting images as to India's state of development. The Indian with whom the American is most likely to interact sees his society as at least well along the road toward industrialization, as regionally powerful, as a proud and competent nation. But the American views India in terms of the shortfall in development according to American standards. In the American's image, India is almost symbolic of the development problem: grinding poverty and a disaster-prone mass population living on the verge of famine. This mismatch of views seems to account for part of the stand-off in relationships that was especially pronounced in the mid-1970s. It has been exacerbated by Americans' image of themselves as advisors and prescribers, and the patron of India's "progress." The Americans' entire experience is one of extending themselves to save the Indian's soul, to educate, stave off disasters, demonstrate how a democracy should work, and make India produce in a modern way. The American has derived a certain satisfaction in playing this role. It is hard to give it up, especially when India has provided one of the world's most inviting targets for activistic beneficence. It is difficult to play less than the superior role—a more balanced relationship would be less ego-satisfying, less interesting.

The modern Indian has severe problems with these American images and perception habits. Despite unsolved difficulties, they know that theirs is a country of advanced science, steel mills, modern universities, and 800 daily newspapers. Perhaps a third of all India, a subsociety of some 200 million people, feel themselves citizens of the modern world—an outlook which does not fit in American stereotype and therefore tends to be overlooked.

The Americans' image of India has easily recognizable roots. The knowledge base is sometimes described as the Rudyard Kipling syndrome, a romantic preparation to see India through the escape literature and adventure tales of "explorers" seeking the exotic and unusual. The American tourist still "explores" India with much the same anticipation. He starts out tuned to perceive selectively that which stands in exciting contrasts—poverty, religious mysticism, teeming humanity, hopefully snakes and tigers, monsoons, cows in the streets, the caste system, temples and idols, ancient and incomprehensible art, fakirs, and the mysterious wisdom of the East. This "mysterious wisdom" even seems to add a certain credibility to the current fad of transcendental meditation.

Some of this image goes back to the missionary effort to save the "heathens," and their shock with Indian ways (*Mother India*). The Christian duty became one of taking India on as the first "white man's burden." There was a fixation on all that contrasted with American values. Americans absorbed the adventures of the wars on the Afghanistan frontier in novels and films. Later came vicarious adventure in settings such as those in *Bhowani Junction*. Today they trap elephants in India via television and "Wild Kingdom." Add a brush with a Hare Krishna group in an American airport and the image seems more real.

Then came India's struggle for independence, the lofty but little understood Gandhi strategy, and the American technical assistance program. The major concern became one of solving Indian problems ranging from curing its diseases, to recommending economic policy, to curbing population growth.

Textbook learning has been of questionable help. The Asia Society recently reviewed some 300 textbooks in use in 1974–75 to determine how Asia comes across to American school children. They concluded that of all the Asian countries considered, treatment of India seemed to reveal the most negative attitudes, disproportionately singling out disease, death, and illiteracy—implying that Indians are not able to handle technology and forgetting to note that India is one of the world's larger industrial powers. What the reviewers called the "Western-Centered Approach" equated Westernization with modernization, implied that the task is to "progress," to catch up with the West; evaluations were made by Western standards. Textbook sources used were Western, rarely Asian. Social institutions were described in terms of impediments to progress. Mysticism was highlighted; India along with other Asian countries was presented as inscrutable or exotic.[3]

Another set of American images relates to the years of their preoccupation with the ideological conflict and the felt priorities of the Cold War era. India was the world's largest democracy—a dependable ally was expected. Instead, Americans found a "neutral," often outspoken critic in the international forum. Such an independent position was judged ungrateful after all the charity and assistance that had been provided and what Americans saw as their constructive leadership in facing world dangers. The history of this dialogue and its treatment in the American press and media have added to the total lens through which Americans have come to view India and things Indian.

These generalizations are somewhat sweeping, but the image psychology described does affect the articulate public in both countries and does impinge on the communication process. The question is how deeply embedded these images are, and how subject they may be to modification by more balanced information. Some observers suggest that unfortunately there is little incentive for the average American to seek a broader understanding. Modern India is simply not as interesting as traditional India, just as modern Wyoming is less interesting than the Wyoming of the cowboy legend. Rites in a temple attract more attention than a bicycle factory or a nuclear plant. And if the American cannot be about the business of saving India, pulling it out of disasters or tutoring Indians in modern ways, why bother? The image he holds now does serve a psychological function in sustaining the ego and reassuring him of the "superiority" of his own society.

Fortunately, much of the government-to-government and

[3]See the Asia Society's summary, *Asia in American Textbooks* (New York, 1976).

institution-to-institution communication with India draws on a supply of people whose experience is extensive and whose images are more complete. American scholars and specialists have been active in India, as was mentioned in an earlier chapter. The Peace Corps has supplied a new source; during the early 1970s when the program was at its height, more than 1,000 volunteers could be found there at a time, typically working in situations close to Indian daily life where observations take on depth and a sense of context. Over the several years of the program's operation the number of these field-educated young people has become substantial, including even the mother of the President of the United States! Americans who lived in India to carry out the technical assistance work, their staffs, and their families constitute another reservoir of American understanding as they make up the alumni of AID, special contract projects, U.N. activities, and Ford Foundation and Rockefeller programs. Children of missionaries, for all the public distortions which came about as a result of the proselytizing effort supply a sometimes forgotten source of expert knowledge. Many grew up there, learned Indian languages, and absorbed much of the scope of Indian life. Our Ambassador to India at the time of this writing, Robert Goheen, is such a case.

IMAGES BY PROJECTION: BLACK–WHITE
RELATIONS IN AMERICA AND IN AFRICA

Another route by which images and misperceptions come to complicate effective communication is that of *projecting* one's own familiar experience and expectations onto another society when superficial cues suggest that the situation is similar. A rather salient example of this, by considerable evidence, is the American view of black–white relations in Africa. We tend to project onto Africa an American frame of reference which includes the civil rights movements and all the concerns with compliance with egalitarian and equal opportunity values that went with the American conception of a democratic society. Particularly on the American black side, African aspirations appear to be parallel, and the tendency is to assume an identity in outlook. Those closer to the scene argue that there is enough of a mismatch in images that communication regarding black–white issues suffers from considerable confusion.

The following discussion is based on the pilot studies in Africa (Kenya, Zambia, and Cameroon, but not South Africa) and observations related particularly to various activities in the educational exchange and information fields. The factors are complex, politically sensitive on both sides, and not easily subject to objective review when the emotions of colonialism in Africa and those of the struggle for equality in the U.S. have to be taken into account. Yet it does appear that Americans have tended to perceive Africans as extensions of their own racial minority, rather than as nationals of other countries with their own cultures, experience, and concerns.

Race relations has been a central concern in projecting official representation and information programs to Africa. The obvious expectation has been that imperfect American practice could be a liability in achieving cordial relationships between black Africa and the United States, most especially if negative propaganda and sensational news reports made the American situation appear worse than it was. Thus, the official effort was to demonstrate the point that America is an integrated, equal-opportunity society, or at least is making rapid progress toward it. The United States Information Agency highlighted the subject. Black Americans were sent abroad as speakers and performing artists, black studies books were placed in USIS libraries, news and feature stories regarding race relations developments in the United States were given priority attention. In other official missions the proportion of black officers was intentionally increased; an entire Peace Corps unit was recruited from black Americans. African leaders were invited on tours of the United States to see for themselves, and Americans typically started to explain the American situation even before they were asked, perhaps appearing to protest too much.

The evidence is that Americans may have been talking to themselves more than they realize, and in the process many have failed to take into account the actual patterns of African concerns and perceptions. It appears that today Africans are not nearly as concerned about racial problems in the United States as Americans expect, and that there is far less sense of common identity on the part of black Africans with black Americans than Americans, and particularly black Americans, have assumed. American problems are distant to Africans. American blacks are first of all Americans who happen to be black rather than blacks who happen to be Americans. Attempts to prove an American sense of racial justice by exhibiting black Americans in embassies and AID Missions or as sponsored official visitors often have been met with suspicion of intent when done in excess or when it was suspected that Africa was being singled out for the exercise. It was judged that American blacks in American missions in Africa who were accomplished and competent communicators could be very effective, probably more so than their white counterparts, but the racial factor was marginal.[4]

[4]Impressions from the pilot studies discussions were reinforced by a case study analysis conducted by Don Leidel, "Black to Black Images—America and Africa," while he was a member of the Department of State Senior Seminar in Foreign Policy, 1973.

On the negative side, there seemed to be a certain potential for black Americans to have special difficulties in establishing cordial relationships. They had higher expectations, and were more frustrated when they found that all Americans are foreign to Africans, themselves included, and that their racial identification made little difference. Further, in many cases Africans are predisposed to be suspicious of out-group blacks—for it is with them that they have their real antagonisms—and especially so if the strange black is overbearing, ostentatious, or arrogant. Unfortunately, many black Americans, especially those who came to Africa in recent years in search of black brotherhood, have been seen in this way.

Do Africans planning to visit the United States have anxieties as to how they will be received? The answer seems to be yes, to a degree. But this tends to be outweighed by more positive expectations regarding professional opportunities and educational resources if the travel is for study, or the chance to see other aspects of the American scene for themselves. It should be recalled that public behavior in the United States has changed significantly, and that the black visitor is much less likely today to encounter situations which he, as a foreigner, sees as negative. On the contrary, as American public behavior is relatively more informal and friendly toward strangers than is the case in most African or European cities, the African visitor often returns home with what Americans might regard as an unrealistically favorable impression. This image seems to be getting around among would-be travellers, along with, unhappily, a new source of anxiety—street violence. Some felt that this is now a more serious concern in contemplating a U.S. visit than fear of racial discourtesy.

Black officers stationed in Africa find that Africans tend to ask them more questions about the American racial situation than are asked of white officers. In turn, white officers are more frequently asked questions regarding the role of black officers in the mission. But it is surprising how little the subject is raised, not how much. Fulbright professors in the countries visited reported that American race relations were rarely raised by their students, even when the course lent itself to it, or when professors intentionally invited discussion.

The obvious but usually neglected task is to capture the contrasting frame of reference by which Africans look at racial matters. To start with, to be black in Africa is not to be a minority. To be a member of a given tribe might be, but to some other black majority, and this of course, is the source of many discontents. But the relationship to whites has been one with foreign outsiders who have imposed themselves as a ruling minority under a wide variety of conditions and standards of behavior toward Africans. Europeans were also missionaries and teachers, and it can be argued that relationships with whites were based more on their brand of colonial behavior than the fact that they were of a different race.

From the point of view of any given tribe, Europeans have not been the only ones to impose themselves by force. Other black tribes did, Arabs did. Slavery, which means so much to black Americans, is less a black–white issue in Africa, where Africans also took slaves and in fact were much involved in selling their fellow blacks to the foreign slavers. It is important to note the obvious fact that Africans are the descendants of those who *stayed behind* and knew little of the overseas slavery that was experienced by New World blacks and has become so important to their identity. Today Africans have little occasion to identify with an issue that is distant in geography and generation.

So race relations in independent black African countries start out as colonial relations, still accompanied with bitterness in most areas over past treatment and the low value placed on the African's worth. Discrimination as such was but one factor, and one of less significance in the face of a primary concern which was to retake the superior and commanding position which homeland and majority status indicated. There was little assumption that they should be integrated into the *minority* white society. Once independence was gained, exploitation and continuing colonialist behavior became the issues. This is a different black–white world than that seen in the United States.

All this is not to hold irrelevant the concern that Americans, black and white, have for exercising constructive American influence in promoting social justice and standards of human rights in Africa. The situation in South Africa is substantially different in any case. The point is that by projecting an image that does not accord with African reality, and by misperceiving events and developments there, the message that Americans try to communicate tends to be lost in the contrast between the ways that the situation and its event are understood on the two sides.

COPING WITH MISPERCEPTIONS
OF THE UNITED STATES ITSELF

However well Americans recognize their myths regarding the rest of the world, and attend to the quality of their misperceptions, there remains the matter of coping with misperceptions that others hold of the United States, its society and culture, and its problems and objectives. Doing something about other peoples' images and understanding has been the long-standing mission of the International Communication Agency and its predecessor, the United States Information Agency. In their travels, private Americans also find themselves trying to straighten out the strange picture of themselves they encounter, images that run the range from Hollywood glamor and cowboys and gangsters to the unrealistically high assumptions of wealth and unlimited opportunity that inspire potential immigrants. Some distortions are to be expected as we are seen from a distance through the limited and imperfect channels available. Others are more deliberately prompted for political, nationalistic or scapegoat reasons—Yankee imperialists, for example.

For most readers, little purpose would be served in reviewing the substance and source of these misperceptions. They are familiar. Rather, several notes on what is involved in meeting the problem would be more germane to the discussion here.

First, the logical procedure here is to recognize that any self-misperception or less-than-accurate images that Americans hold of themselves have to be entered into the equation. It is difficult to evaluate foreign distorted impressions through an unevaluated and subjective set of lenses. It is even possible, although we will resist the thought, that the outsiders' views that we term misperceptions might actually be more detached and accurate than our own. Potentially there is a kind of objectivity to be gained from a foreign vantage point that is not possible when one is too close to one's own society and its events. In fact, one of the fringe benefits for many Americans living abroad and experiencing contrasts is the enlarged perspective that they can gain of their own country.

Dialogue based on the combination of both a foreign and a self-misperception is an exercise in futility, yet this is what is happening more often than is realized. In the next chapter this will be explored in more detail for its relation to foreign affairs decision-making. However, if Americans are to play a responsible leadership role in making international communication a more rational and dependable process, they will have to find a way to take into account their own ethnocentricity factor as part of their operating conceptions regarding the U.S. No breast-beating is required, just a practical attempt at objectivity. Some samples: the United States is probably not as much of a free enterprise society as Americans think; government constraints in the public interest rival those in societies that may describe themselves differently. American society is not as much the open-class system in which rugged individualism, initiative, and self-reliance are the way to the top as the American dream would indicate. Welfare has become a way of life for some, and much of the society looks to government to reduce their risks: unemployment compensation, social security, national medical plans, perhaps guaranteed income. Conflicting values place many Americans in awkward positions. It is difficult to be poor with dignity in the United States because the society still says that one *ought* to achieve and move up the social ladder when much of the population cannot be that much in control of their own circumstances. Negative self-images may be wrong also. On balance, the United States may not be as violent and as dangerous a society as an efficient and sensational media would make it appear.

Second, if a highly interdependent world calls for more problem-solving communication, a distinction will have to be made between the utility of a *favorable* image versus an *accurate* image. Some observers suggest that within the American national character there is a comparatively pronounced need to be liked, and with that a preoccupation with foreign public opinion polls or other indicators of current popularity. Certainly this is where the USIA research effort has gone for many years. (The new ICA is researching much more fundamental aspects of the communication environment.) While there would seem to be no virtue in being *disliked*, the more important question in the future may be whether the United States is *accurately* understood, whether its actions are predictable and seem consistent rather than capricious. Sometimes the most reasonable expectation may be that the United States be respected, and that by being comprehended, will be able to exercise the leadership role that is commensurate with its power and position.

It follows that consideration must be given to just what it is that leads to a more accurate image. Little analytical thought has been given to this question; many of the activities intended to improve the American image abroad have been either conceived as public relations programs or have concentrated more on the mechanism than the substance. One particularly unanalyzed notion is that simply to see the United States at first-hand—to visit this country or to meet us more often—is to like us and understand us. If foreign critics could visit and see for themselves, their misperceptions would vanish. Obviously the potential is there, and this has been the result in many instances. But this is naive, for changes in perception and opinion do not take place so simply. The way that such new experience is processed depends on the existing frame of reference; misunderstanding could even be fortified as the visitor perceives what he is already programmed to see. Somewhat the same process is involved in attempts to project the American scene abroad by exhibits, art, ballet performances, films, even American studies.

Thus, especially if the attention shifts to the communicating elites and more *accurate* understanding, more precision will be needed in identifying just where the key comprehension gaps are. It will be especially important to know which fundamental conceptions held of the United States are so out of focus as to make it difficult to capture the logic and pattern of American society and culture, and therefore to make sense of its details. The real difficulty is that what the foreign observer needs to understand is precisely that which the American is least likely to try to explain, for the logic of American life is carried implicitly and out of awareness—it is the "obvious," the usual, the common sense, that which is taken for granted. If one is to explain to a foreign visitor, there is always more to be said than to another American: it is *why* a given custom or practice makes sense to the American that needs to be clarified. It may be easy to explain the technical aspects of voting or setting the high school curriculum, for example, or how the mayor's budget works. But it is much harder, and much more important, to explain the patterns of thinking, the values, and the implicit assumptions which lie behind the practice and behavior. Unhappily, the prospects are poor at best; the only sure way is for the foreign observer to seek reincarnation as an American, and absorb it all in growing up. If the cultural difference is substantial, the difficulties are the greater, of course.

Finally, for a growing number of elites, bilateral understanding is not enough, particularly when the subjects of dialogue are those of international interaction—military assistance, economic institutions, etc. In these matters the United States cannot be understood in isolation, or simply in the bilateral relationship. Thus, it would be easier to correct some highly important misperceptions, such as those regarding foreign policy positions, if a way could be found to enlarge the global perspective and understanding of a vastly increasing number of people and groups who will be the key communicators in a more global society. The case can be made that the United States, in its efforts to exert responsible leadership in international communication, would be acting in its own interest in supporting activities that lead to an enlarged global literacy and perspective *abroad* as well as at home.

"NOISE" IN COMMUNICATION RELATIONSHIPS

Communication analysts often find it useful to identify background factors or elements in a communication situation which are extraneous to the central exchange but which tend to prevent the listener from "hearing" the message. This they have called "noise." The problem might literally be distracting noise; it might be a nervous tic, cigar smoke, the presence of other people, or the memory of a previous upsetting disagreement with the person now trying to transmit a message. There might be an endless list of such items which conceivably could impinge on the perception and assigned meaning of the communication content.

In cross-cultural communication, possibilities for distracting noise are enlarged considerably. Style, accents, gestures, anxieties in ill-

defined situations make their impact. One of the distractions most familiar to readers who have followed the intercultural communication field is
the simple matter of how far apart people normally stand in informal
conversation.[5] This is learned out of awareness. For Americans it is
about an arm's length; in the Middle East the distance is typically much
less. One is unconscious of this factor until the cross-cultural encounter
is experienced. Then this difference in patterned behavior can make so
much "noise" that communication is subject to a whole range of misperceptions and images. If too close, a person is pushy and aggressive; if too
far the person may be overly cold, untrusting, unfriendly. The list of
such items goes on and on. Thais giggle too much. Americans chew gum,
are too loud and unreserved. Some Africans will not look you in the eye.

Items such as these lead to a sense of social distance, emotional
discomfort, and misattributions of character and motive. This is a broad
field of both serious study and entertaining conversation. The problem,
in the interest of international communication, is to build up a much
greater public understanding of these factors so that they are anticipated
and given more accurate meaning. In this way their effect as "noise" can
be better taken into account for more successful mutual adaptation. This
is sometimes included in higher quality language teaching, especially
when the idea is to teach the student to *communicate* rather than simply to
speak. It is also one of the concerns of a growing group of professionals
in intercultural communication now joining forces in a new organization, the Society for Intercultural Education, Training, and Research.

The implications of this dimension for misperception and image
distortions can be further illustrated in the case of Americans and South
Asians, especially Indians in the United States. More careful research
and analysis is needed, but it widely agreed that there is a pronounced
amount of noise in this relationship, some that goes beyond the more
general factors considered above. Americans start with a feeling of social
distance, empathy comes slowly. Unhappily, in the broad range of
nationalities that visit the U.S., Indians are often seen as the most "difficult," those hosted with the least enthusiasm. Even Americans with
long association with them and with close Indian friends recognize the
pattern. If the elements could be satisfactorily identified and understood, perhaps the noise could be coped with more constructively. Ten-
tatively, the direction of inquiry might go as follows:

First, problems in social interaction: despite the many exceptions,
to many Americans, Indian visitors tend to come off as demanding,
quickly critical, cold, arrogant, and nit-pickingly argumentative. In-

---

[5] This standard illustration goes back to the observations of Edward T. Hall, *The
Silent Language* (Garden City, N.Y.: Doubleday, 1959).

terestingly, Americans in India experience less of this feeling unless they are tangled up in the Indian bureaucracy.

Why should the "chemistry" be so difficult in the American–Indian case? Part of the problem seems to be a mismatch of perceptions of social hierarchy and the behavior which is expected to go with differences in status and role. As noted in another context in the last chapter, despite good intentions, adjustment to American subtleties of egalitarianism is difficult after being socialized in India's more rigid structure where one is accustomed to deferring to or being deferred to. Americans particularly resent someone who signals that he should be deferred to, especially in social settings.[6]

Possibly there is also a mismatch in style of discussion and debate. The Indian predilection is to take a firm position and defend it; the American likes informal give-and-take and inductive examination of the evidence, and seeks a compromised or agreed position. This aspect of dialogue may be made more difficult by the intonation patterns the Indian carries in his use of English, a combination of a British accent and the hard and precise speech patterns carried over from a number of Indian languages that together have the effect of sounding more overbearing and humorless to the American than intended. Without knowing quite why, the American feels a tenseness in the atmosphere, is unable to feel at ease in the conversation or feel that it is a friendly exchange. Conversation has a way of becoming a confrontation. In turn, the American's reluctance to use titles or show deference when deemed due is seen as lack of respect and rudeness, a stance which seems to take the visitor for granted or demean him.

Some observers believe that a highly complicated anxiety regarding racial identity on the part of the Indian often contributes to the "noise." There is a patterned sensitivity to degrees of racial differentiations, often going back to Indian society itself, and to memories of colonial experience. This is made more difficult by ambiguity on the American side; the pattern in race relations seems inconsistent and unpredictable to the Indian. Some Americans feel that Indians can be more hypersensitive than African visitors, perhaps because the Indian feels caught in the middle in racial identities. It may not be so much a worry that nonegalitarian racial distinctions might be drawn, but that someone will make a mistake in his case. Given the already complicated notion of status distinctions which do not fit American society, adding the nuances of ill-defined racial considerations simply overloads the system. Actually, we know very little about this set of outlooks. Indeed, it may vary consid-

----

[6]This problem area was explored in cooperation with the Indian community in Chicago by University of Chicago anthropologist, Ralph Nicholas. Discussion with him contributed to this tentative explanation.

erably depending on specific Indian ethnic subgroups, and of course by individual. In any case, the sensitivity is sufficient to lead the Indian to suspect racial slights out of proportion to their actuality, or to think that he is receiving a cool reception because of race when other factors are the cause.

Thus one could pursue the distracting factors. Indian attire when used in the United States is almost symbolic of foreignness—the turban, and the sari which Indian women tend to retain long after their husbands have adopted western suits. Then there is the reservation in the back of the American's mind regarding profound religious differences, even though in fact many Indian visitors, and especially members of the resident Indian community, may be Christians. This aspect of cultural difference makes it harder to empathize with them than with Latin Americans or Europeans, or even Muslims. The fact that some Americans have turned to variants of Indian religion and philosophy, especially groups already suspect for their counter-culture ways, may make the mainstream American extra-sensitive to the Indian's religious identification. That is, what is seen as deviant *American* behavior tends to feed back to make the *Indians* more suspect. At the least there is enough of an aura of this possibility that the Indian community in the United States looks on American faddists of Indian religions with some anxiety as a liability in their own public relations.

It is worth noting that present performance in supporting research and study in the intercultural communication field leaves much to be desired. It deserves much higher priority, both by the institutions which should invest in the endeavor and by the social scientists who have the special competence. Cultural anthropologists, for example, have been remarkably inattentive to this application of their discipline. Few sociologists or social psychologists work with international or cross-cultural processes. And interdisciplinary work in this field is even less developed. The remedy in part would be more effort to define clearly the areas in which research is needed, and of course to provide the financial backing that is the indispensable stimulus. Those who are now carrying the burden in expanding both basic and applied knowledge are doing so more by conviction than by visible support. Many come from the communication, training and bilingual education fields. The Culture Learning Institute at the East–West Center in Honolulu has been an important and productive locus for advancing the field.

7

CONSIDERING THE COMMUNICATION
DIMENSION IN THE CONDUCT
OF FOREIGN AFFAIRS

Inevitably, rapid change in international communication processes is having a profound effect on the way nations conduct their foreign affairs. This has been amply evident in virtually all of the most significant recent international developments. In the case of President Sadat's historic 1977 visit to Israel, television's search for media events may have been the precipitating factor. Leaders and statesmen are well advanced in taking communication considerations into account either to avoid having their problems compounded by communication repercussions, or to use communication potential to their advantage.

However, beyond the big events, the communication revolution affects the routine business of foreign affairs institutions. This requires new ways of thinking about the communication dimension and new ways of working with it, most especially in government. Therefore the question: how can government equip itself to handle communication factors in the era ahead? As the United States is the nation with the greatest communication activity and impact, the U.S. Government would seem to carry a special responsibility, both to its own constituents and to the rest of the world. Whether this disproportionate influence is managed with vision and wisdom or not, its performance will be a matter of deep world concern for the remainder of this century.

At the least, government will have to expand its conception of the relevance of international communication processes to international relations, and thereby direct greater effort toward understanding and managing them. Certainly the communication process cannot simply be taken for granted as a neutral and mechanical aspect of international interaction, nor as of concern only when public relations endeavors are to be conducted. It has to be considered in its own right as a proper *subject* of international relations analysis, and government will have to give more studied attention to conducting United States international *communication* relations. There will need to be a new capacity to deal with international communication affairs, just as there is for international economic, security, political, or development affairs.

Without overdramatizing this by talking in terms of crises or turning points, it can still be argued that changing circumstances do come together forcefully enough to suggest some urgency for taking cognizance of trends and new factors. Consider, by way of summary, the situation produced in the combination of the following sample items:

—Communication, and access to it, has become an essential world "commodity" vital to all nations. The equipment and technology side is fundamental, but the larger interest is in the flow of messages and information. It is this part that is increasingly seen as essential "goods and services" to be managed equitably and with consideration for the needs of the various members of the international community.

—Diplomacy itself, the way in which policies are arrived at and the way they actually work out, are all increasingly dependent on the way that publics obtain information, perceive issues, reason about them, form opinions, and bring pressure to bear. The future will be even more of an era of public diplomacy, which is, of course, a communication process. The decision maker, therefore, has even greater reason to take the communication dimension into account *before* decisions are reached, rather than simply look to it *afterward* for public relations purposes.

—With the large increase in the total number of nations now taking part in international affairs, government has to manage a correspondingly larger and more complicated set of communications relations. The problem is compounded as new nations with contrasting cultures and national experiences experiment with new political and economic approaches in their national development and in their interface with other nations. Messages now fly around among more than 150 nations, not counting all the subdivisions and separate cultural and interest groups involved.

—Communication *per se* has already become the *substance* of international debate and negotiation as vested communication interests come into conflict. This appears in bilateral relations, as with Canada, and in multilateral forums, such as UNESCO and meetings of nonaligned states. Some of this debate centers on technological management: the allocation of frequencies, or determining how satellite capabilities will be used. But news flow and the impact one culture has on another via international media have particularly broad political repercussions.

—The efforts of governments in open societies to use communication channels for international public relations or image enhancement purposes have become less relevant as such efforts are increasingly diluted in ever larger streams of other media content that bypasses governmental influence. What governments put into the traffic in the form of information programs or exchange activities becomes proportionately less significant when the whole spectrum of communication is taken into consideration.

—United States ideological and moral advocacy as injected in its international communication is due for new analysis and updating. The phasing out of the Cold War, an American pause for introspection, and resistance to the prescriptive approach abroad has made some of the previous American style of persuasion obsolete. As the U.S. ideological and moral stance has been a unique and powerful element of its presence in world affairs, this rearticulation should be a priority concern in the conduct of American international communication relations.

—As an ever larger number of governmental departments and agencies communicate internationally through their separate activities, negotiations, policies, or sponsored travel and exchange programs, the coordination task for achieving any kind of coherent U.S. thrust in international communication becomes greater. And the need to accomplish it becomes correspondingly more urgent.

—A larger and increasingly significant part of the total international relations process is now conducted by nongovernmental transnational groups and organizations. Their success too depends on communication capabilities. In the national interest, government bears a responsibility for enhancing the conditions and facilities by which such transnational groups are able to communicate effectively abroad.

—It is becoming increasingly apparent that as the well-being of ordinary citizens depends ever more directly on factors outside the U.S., promoting their international education and global perspective will be a national concern. Further, this will be necessary if a democratic society is to support intelligently the deliberations of its own government. Hence, governmental leadership and support for international education becomes a vital aspect of the overall international communication task.

Even these few considerations suggest that tending to the nation's capacity to communicate internationally may become one of the normal and expected concerns of government, along with such familiar ones as providing for the public safety and the regulation of interstate commerce. In the next section we will discuss the government's resources for its own communicating.

THE HIGH PRICE OF MISPERCEPTION
IN GOVERNMENT DECISION-MAKING

In the last chapter we called attention to the damage done by misperception and distorted images. Certainly as government conducts the nation's international business, much depends on how well potential communication pitfalls have been taken into consideration in the many stages of information gathering, analysis, deliberation, decision-making and negotiation. Perhaps the government's ability to cope with misperceptions and misattributions of motive is the most far-reaching concern in the many facets of coping with international communication.

This point appears sufficiently obvious, especially in the context of this discussion. Yet it is not actually the subject of much specific attention, and by all evidence the U.S. government establishment is not well prepared to come to grips with it. It rarely even recognizes that there is a problem, for the managers which emerge from the career service or the political field tend to be very sure of their own conventional wisdom and the dependability of their world-view. While it is standard procedure to turn to science and tested analytical procedures for enhancing performance in military logistics or management, or even in running the credit union, those dealing with foreign affairs problems tend to rely staunchly on their own "common sense" observational and judgmental skills despite the warning signals that they are venturing onto unfamiliar ground where more specialized experience and even scientific help should be sought. It is the mentality that will use computer cross-checking to extend the capacities of the mind in order to manipulate data for making airline reservations or to diagnose a disease, but seeks no objective means to check the accuracy of perceptions of foreign events or to verify an image of another nation's pattern of behavior. It is an approach by which an institution goes to great lengths to check the technical qualifications of a candidate to do a skilled job in an overseas program, but pays no attention to preparation to do that job in a foreign environment.

There is ample evidence that a high price has been paid for such a self-assured but unstudied approach, and that misperception and reasoning on the basis of limited understanding have been at the root of serious foreign affairs miscalculations. The most recent, of course, has been the Viet Nam adventure which has left even some of those who are still convinced that there was need for that invervention admitting that the right questions about Viet Nam were not asked and that the cultural reality had not been taken into account. It is clear after the fact that American governmental decision-makers did not have the kind of area experience or available knowledge to make reliable judgments about events unfolding there. In some cases they lacked even the awareness that the cultural and societal difference in that part of the world should prompt them to use the expert knowledge that was available—especially when that expert counsel seemed to go against American conventional assumptions about the cause and development of communist-identified political movements. Perhaps even worse, since the end of the conflict there has been more inclination to "put Viet Nam behind us" than to seek the lessons that might be learned.

Our limited inclination to learn to take public psychological factors into account was evident again in the case of Iran. As in Viet Nam, a self-assured topside of the government's policy-making institution gave low priority to factoring into their day-to-day deliberations the special qualities of Iranian social, and especially religious reality. Thus, again, a series of decisions over the years which seemed in each case to make common sense added up to an erroneous total.

Courageously pursuing far-reaching actions on the basis of uncorrected misperceptions is not a new shortcoming, nor is it a practice confined to Americans. For example, John Stoessinger in his *Nations in Darkness* (1971) takes a long look back at the key decisions taken by the United States, Russia, and China in the course of their interaction as nations. He has found that an alarmingly large portion of these decisions on all sides were based on serious misperceptions. There were misperceptions on the part of decision-makers themselves and also by their publics. There were misperceptions of the other's intentions and power, and self-misperceptions too. Sometimes favorable intentions were seen when they did not exist, but more typically the reverse was the case. In looking back over history Stoessinger reminds us of Krushchev's misperception of the resolve of the new Kennedy administration in 1962 before the Cuban Missile Crisis, and documents the American public's misreading of Chiang Kai-shek's leadership in China as heroic, irresistible, Christian and pro-American. He notes that the legend of help from the presence of the Russian fleet in New York and San Francisco during the War between the States that left a glow of good feeling toward the Russians for the next half century was a misperception. The Russian presence had nothing to do with the Americans' troubles, but was an escape from British and French fleets with whom they had other problems. Then there was the more recent erroneous assumption of Russian–Chinese solidarity, which actually had long been clouded by mutual suspicions and misperceptions.

The problem comes into sharp focus in reviewing the dramatic misperception by which the Bay of Pigs invasion was attempted in Cuba. In retrospect it is clear that the planners simply saw in the Cuban situation what they wanted to see—and what turned out not to be there: intense Cuban dissatisfaction with the Castro regime, chafing under Communist rule, a widespread willingness to take high risks to overthrow the oppression. Actually, some contrary, more objectively derived, evidence was available to the Kennedy White House at the time. An experienced specialist in public opinion analysis had arranged, with understandable difficulty, a public opinion survey in Cuba. This indicated that by far the larger part of the Cuban people was either reasonably content with the Castro regime, or at least seemed not unhappy enough to risk doing anything about it. In short, this American performance in failing to recognize and cope with misperceptions in the Bay of Pigs fiasco did not enhance American credibility or add confidence in any American pretense at communication leadership.

Unhappily, such case examples could be cited at length—the misperceptions of Chinese intentions in Korea in 1950, of the motivations of contending groups in Angola in 1976, of the Japanese "shock" at American procedures in renewing contact with China in 1971, of an American "need" to demonstrate its power in the Mayaguez incident in 1975. More fortunately, a growing group in foreign affairs circles is now coming to recognize the misperception danger, and the academic community also has become much more concerned. For instance, this well-accepted title—*Perception and Misperception in International Politics* (1976) by Robert Jervis—indicates growing interest in psychological problems and processes in international relations decisions. (The book does not, however, venture far into the cross-cultural factors that make the perception process so different in various parts of the world.)

Tracing the causes of misperception through the government deliberation process is relatively easy. One can point quickly to some of the main contributing factors. The first is insufficient knowledge base. Too many in the decision-making chain arrive at their conclusions with too little in-depth information of the foreign nations to which the problem at hand relates. Actually, the difficulty in commanding sufficient knowledge is inherently greater for Americans, for by being so central a power many American officials too often have to switch their attention across a range of dozens of nations. A decision-maker in a less extensively involved country would have an easier task—perhaps understanding 10 to 15 countries would serve his purpose. Also, American decision-makers tend to be highly specialized, not in an area of the world, but in a given substantive field such as law of the sea or aviation agreements. Their interest in any particular country is thus narrow, and the effort that would be required to pursue their special interest through its full context of meaning for all the countries with which they must deal would be considerable. When the need arises, they too typically have to rely on "what I read in the newspapers." Even the career Foreign Service Officers who might supply a generalist function tend to become specialists also as foreign problems become more technically demanding. In any case, they are spread very thinly in government, and even in overseas missions.

The problem is compounded as more internationally relevant decisions are made in departments or agencies that are essentially organized to perform domestic missions, such as the Departments of Agriculture, Treasury, or Justice. Their staffs are oriented to see the internal, not the international, effects of what they do. They are less likely to anticipate the public diplomacy consequences that their decisions will have as they reverberate in other countries or be sensitive to the significance of changing social and psychological factors.

Unfortunately, the people whose judgments enter into decisions find that there is less opportunity than might be expected for their background comprehension to grow rapidly in service. Even the intelligence resources to which foreign affairs officers might turn for help tend to become specialized around problems and issues. Relatively little of the intelligence or research effort is directed toward supplying generalized contextual explanation. So decision-makers start out on their own with only the proverbial blind man's view of the elephant. They have little chance of gaining fully accurate perceptions or of coming to totally balanced conclusions.

What the decision-maker inevitably does, then, is *project* a sense of context onto the situation, as noted in the last chapter. And the normal context to project would be one's own. A sobering study made in the Central Intelligence Agency, now declassified, demonstrates how intelligence analysts, the very people most relied on for objective explanations of foreign developments, are also victims of the projection process. Marc Lewis (1976), after reviewing intelligence reports produced during two critical periods of American involvement in Viet Nam, believes that hidden assumptions produce a critical vulnerability to serious error. For example, in the reports Viet Nam President Ngo Dinh Diem was noted to be "irreproachably nationalist, unprecedently honest," and "genuinely anti-Communist," but little attention was paid to the cultural factors or Vietnamese patterns of thinking which would establish how power is shared, exercised, or retained—the factors which would determine how

Diem would actually fare as a leader in that society. Thus, when conceptualized in American terms, the analysts were not able to give their
readers a reliable basis for anticipating his inability to provide the leadership necessary to combat insurgent forces. Again, better information *was*
available, but it did not make comfortable sense to American analysts,
who carried their own reality worlds into their analysis task.[1]

Sometimes the problem of accurate perception is exacerbated by
the group processes through which so many American decisions are
made. This is summed up in a title used by Irving Janis: *Victims of Group
Think* (1972). In this book he notes how all the subtleties of protecting
group solidarity, taking assurance from group consensus, avoiding the
appearance of being a deviant, and so on, combine to exclude conflicting
evidence and give group-derived decisions a sense of reliability that is
not merited. Sometimes, in fact, decisions are reached that no member
of the group would have felt comfortable with on his own. Janis thinks
that some of the success in the process by which decisions were made
during the Cuban Missile Crisis was due to procedures that helped break
the hypnotic group effect.

But the very essence of government decision-making is that the
product has to make sense to groups of people—groups within agencies,
political groups that support an administration, ultimately the American
public. This makes difficult any deliberation process calculated to cut
through the images that are molded by an American cultural base and
are reinforced by information channels that also reflect these ethnocentric patterns of perception.

Thus, the society that prides itself on applied science, the people
who require thorough scientific testing before any new drug is placed on
the market, will allow their foreign affairs decision-makers to practice on
the basis of their intuition and informal judgment. This would seem to
be one of the frontiers of applied knowledge yet to be conquered in the
last part of the twentieth century.

WHAT MISSION FOR THE
INTERNATIONAL COMMUNICATION
AGENCY?

The new governmental entity, the International Communication Agency (ICA), has come into being just as the need for a more
studied government role in United States communication relations has

---

[1]For an easily available summary, see Marc Lewis, "The Blind Spot of U.S. Foreign
Intelligence," *Journal of Communication* (Winter, 1976).

become more apparent. How "new" it will be depends on how completely the conception of its mission is updated. Bureaucratically it combines the former United States Information Agency (called a Service abroad), the Voice of America, and the Department of State's Bureau of Educational and Cultural Affairs (called CU in bureaucratese). To the extent that ICA does assume a fresh sense of mission and function, it may be the first really new hold taken to manage the official side of American communication abroad since its parent agencies gelled in the early post-World War II years.

The question is whether a combination of institutional lag and a lack of a clearly updated mandate will lead instead to simply repackaging the same activities. Established bureaucrats, like generals, tend to keep on fighting the last war, reusing the same ideas. Ideally, the approach in setting a new mission would be to adopt the zero-based budget technique, but in ideas rather than in dollars, proceeding as if a new agency were being formed to serve the functions required from 1978 onward. This is not easy. Consensus does not crystallize so quickly either within or without an organization, and in any event it is a tricky business to determine just what communication mission a government agency is to presume to perform for a democratic society. The one element which does signal a new thrust is the president's March, 1978 directive to ICA to play a central role in building *two-way* bridges of understanding between Americans and other peoples of the world. He emphasized the American need to gain the kind of understanding of other countries that would contribute to the capacity of both the U.S. people and government to manage foreign affairs with sensitivity, effectiveness and responsibility. This strengthens what had already been a loosely-defined part of the former CU mission, and adds a complementing objective to the established USIA purpose to inform the rest of the world about the United States and the way it works. Thus, from a previous range of program activities—including serving as the information arm overseas for the U.S. government and its embassies, the Fulbright academic exchange, cultural exchange, selection and programming official visitors, operating libraries and giving English classes abroad, presenting exhibits, counselling on American university admissions requirements, and operating the radio voice of the U.S.—a new integration of programs is being designed.

It is beyond the scope of this study to try either to describe all this activity or to propose a mission statement for this new incarnation. Even in looking at certain key factors bearing on the ICA mission, discussion will be skewed somewhat toward the developing world as that is the main "data base" for this study. Still, while recognizing that the view here is not a 360 degree one, certain observations may help the reader pose the issues which this Agency will face as it addresses itself to a new era of communication tasks.

A first question is whether ICA is to be thought of simply as a "service" in the sense of being an institution that supplies the managers and technicians to carry out information or cultural exchange duties that have been decided upon by other policy-makers. Or is it to be upgraded to become that part of the executive branch that actually takes charge of conducting United States communication relations? This might appear to be a fine point of interest mostly to the officers who have to fight Washington bureaucratic battles. But the basic issue is whether the government gives the conduct of international communication relations the stature that it deserves today in the total international relations process. It can be argued that in the national interest it might be as appropriate to have a *Department* of Communication as one dealing with Energy or Transportation. The implication would be that the mandate to manage the official side of United States communication relations is a much more timely conception of mission than merely being the government's public relations arm abroad.

Updating and upgrading the conception of ICA could help define its function in today's world. In the government establishment and in the public mind, expectations for the Agency could expand from the rather simplistic and woefully undefined assignment to "tell America's story to the world" and to "promote mutual understanding" to the premise that the Agency represents the government's primary capability for leading the country in the conduct of its official communication relations with the rest of the world, and for enhancing the means and the public readiness for conducting nonofficial communication relations as well.

It should be recognized that even before reorganization, both USIA and the Bureau of Educational and Cultural Affairs had made significant adjustments in the logic of their programs to fit the changing international communication environment. For example, USIA had taken into account the vast increase in information channels that reach their foreign audiences, and accordingly had more sharply defined their own audiences and the purpose of their programs. Overseas libraries now serve more specialized users. More attention is directed toward longer-range comprehension of the United States and less to superficial propaganda. CU had already exercised increasing leadership in urging American attention to the domestic need for international education and had turned the thrust of its international visitor programs (in the U.S.) from show-and-tell tours to occasions for multilateral dialogue on contemporary world problems. More concern had been directed toward the quality of educational experience that the many foreign students in the United States will have. A larger part of the effort has gone into facilitating formation of new transnational linkages, and toward the need to supply more exchange opportunities for elites other than those in the traditional educational world.

Still, reorganization presents the opportunity to rethink the mission, to stand back and reexamine the logic, to ask what kind of official communication programs respond to the needs of a crowded world. Such a review might indicate that certain established activities should go on, but because they continue to serve a function *now* rather than because of institutional entrenchment. Most important, a full review could open the door to a pursuit of new objectives appropriate to needs of the future rather than those of the past.

To be sure, certain basic ICA responsibilities as the government's communication team do go on. It has a set of highly practical functions to perform overseas that are demanding, required skilled professionals, and need support from Washington. The problem in carrying them out is to avoid letting daily routine and logistics become so time-consuming that no energy is left over for pursuing broader international communication purposes. But a fundamental workload is there. An embassy needs to supply information and answer questions; it needs a competent press officer. There are diplomatic and intergovernmental matters to attend to in the educational, artistic, or public relations field. This is especially so as these activities become more official in many countries where government assumes basic responsibility in their Ministries of Culture or Education. Even shipping an art exhibit or sending a dance team to the U.S. will require some governmental role, if only to issue visas. U.S. cultural presentations are handy for good relations with a local public, or in the diplomatic community. And foreign service reporting, analysis, and negotiation often involve considerations related to the communication field. For example, there might be a need to consider the political role of the local press, or a UNESCO issue. Hence, the career diplomatic officer with a communication and information specialty is a standard member of an embassy team in American, as well as in other official representations.

But if the conception of ICA is to expand toward its being the government's central institution responsible for managing the official international communication relations of the U.S., ICA should be expected to take the lead in defining communication issues for the rest of the government establishment. The opposite has usually been the case. With that responsibility, it would have to look to its analytical competence to identify the salient trends and factors that affect communication relations, to indicate where the dialogue needs reinforcing, to note clearly where misperceptions on both sides are inhibiting effective mutual understanding, and to spell out just what these misperceptions are. It would need to become the nation's experts on the dynamics of news and information flow and the international repercussions that have to be considered. It would need to be able to give advice on how communications issues fit into the total scheme of international affairs, just as defense or commercial specialists would expect to do that for their areas of responsibility.

It follows that a way needs to be found for the professionals in international communication to be part of the international policy decision-making process itself, and be able to inject their analysis and recommendations at the genesis stage. Virtually every important future international decision will have a communications component. Identifying what that is in the course of deliberation is essential. This would be one of the key changes called for in a new conception for ICA if it is not to be simply a public relations effort or a mechanism to make the best of a situation after the fact. As expressed by the late Edward R. Murrow when he directed USIA and urged this role, the agency should be in on the take-off, not just the crash landings.

The impediment to such a purposeful assignment for ICA is that the rest of the international affairs community holds a rather limited view of the importance of the communication dimension, or assumes that communication considerations are obvious enough that reasonable and intelligent people can deal with them without special experience or analytical tools. The view is that the communication professional is needed only for the technical jobs of packaging and transmitting policy information and justification, perhaps for choosing the best slant for optimum persuasion abroad. They fail to see that, as Alexander Kendrick (1967) put it in his biography of Edward R. Murrow, "skillful propagation of poor policy would merely intensify error."

So those who follow foreign affairs have heretofore come to see the communication specialist as the professional propagandist—necessary, but best kept at a distance from the real world of international business, and kept at an even greater distance from the American public. The issue for the future is the degree to which ICA should continue to base its activities on advocacy as has been understood to be the function of USIA, at least in the public and congressional mind. This debate has already commanded serious and measured consideration in the case of the Voice of America. The consensus is well advanced that the Voice serves American interests best when it informs most reliably and credibly. In fact, in bringing the VOA into ICA there had to be assurance that it could continue to operate on this basis so that VOA supporters would acquiesce. Logically, ICA will still be the part of government operations primarily responsible for such advocacy as is pursued. But as accurate and reliable mutual understanding is seen to be the objective, ICA will need to seek new criteria for measuring success. Criteria will no longer be the size of audience turnout, the number of people "reached," the applause, or the improved image or popularity of the United States. It will not be volume of communication, but the quality and reliability of it. This will be hard to measure—a fact that both ICA and its public at home will have to have the wisdom to accept.

This means that part of the new conception will be a realization of what ICA should *not* be. Presumably it is no longer an instrument of the Cold War or a mechanism to manipulate youth toward a favorable orientation toward the United States and all it stands for. It is not America's agent in a popularity contest, nor the salesman that tries to urge developing nations to buy American institutions from an American catalog. It is not the peacetime voice of negative propaganda that intentionally distorts the image of other nations for short-range tactical advantage. And realistically, it will not be an arm of government machinery with a capacity to contrive a receptive ambience for the execution of U.S. foreign policy, especially a foreign policy that has not taken the public communication realities of that ambience into consideration in the first place. Its future ability to persuade will be more a product of its credibility, its capacity for adding missing information in the interest of accuracy and a fuller comprehension of American methods and objectives, and its contribution to the health of the larger information and image flow of which ICA is only a part.[2]

One of the challenges posed for meeting the communication demands of a changing environment is to put more specific and updated meaning into the catch phrases by which much previous activity has been conducted. A prime example is "mutual understanding." Like cleanliness, this is not easily questioned; programs to promote it are always worth at least pro forma support. But what does it mean—especially as applied to ICA? To the public, and often to Congress and much of officialdom looking on from the sidelines, expectations are hazy. Even when it first became an official objective, as in the early days of the Fulbright and related cultural exchange programs, it was a very general affirmation of faith. Exchange among elites and futures elites would result in a better base of public preconceptions for approaching and resolving the problems which rise in the normal interaction of nations and peoples.

Exchange programs were seen as a means for producing an essen-

---

[2]A partial examination of an updated mission for the agencies that eventually became the International Communication Agency was made by a public commission headed by Frank Stanton. Its report supplies useful background. See *International Information, Education, and Cultural Relations: Recommendations for the Future* (Washington, D.C.: Center for Strategic and International Studies, 1975).

tial degree of empathy and for reducing needless misperception of the other side and its intentions. Also, there was mutual advantage to be gained in recognizing and sharing knowledge and cultural achievement, especially in the early post-war world when mutual understanding applied to nations which enjoyed some degree of equal stature in the exchange process. We have noted earlier that with more attention to relationships with the developing world, "mutual understanding" became more of a one-way street, with knowledge transfer and techniques for knowledge application more the purpose. The Cold War took mutual understanding in governmental programs still further in a one-way mode, the idea being that the rest of the world should understand the United States.

Now ICA faces the problem of getting mutual understanding onto a formulation that makes sense in a new communication arena.[3] One pressing question for ICA will be how to engender quality understanding on the part of its own public—the American people, particularly key Americans who will become involved in international matters. ICA has a special problem, for there is no American national Ministry of Education or state broadcasting system to work with, and no likelihood that there will be, given the American system of values. Creation of ICA raises this issue, for USIA was prohibited from distributing its materials, even its best films, in the United States itself, while CU was given the mandate to promote *mutual* understanding. Especially in the latter years of its independent existence, it sought increasingly to find ways to encourage and facilitate the American learning process. CU officers worried that the heavy one-way flow that had developed in exchange activities was detrimental to Americans. It wasted their opportunity to profit from such exchange activities as could be sustained in limited budgets and programs.

Hence, new programs directed toward quality *mutual* understanding will need to seek ways to be more selective in choosing participants, particularly American participants. Presumably ICA will not have to be the organization to supply technical assistance advisors, but the one that gives Americans, too, an opportunity to better comprehend the foreign world and expand their perspectives to match the global society in which they live.

There is a possibility that the Fulbright program has been overtaken by events, or that if it were being established now, it would have more specific mutual understanding purposes. Its current function has

---

[3]For a thoughtful review of what mutual understanding means by one who was responsible for administering government programs toward that end, see John Richardson, Jr., "Mutual Understanding Revisited," *Exchange* (Summer, 1975). Richardson also edited the March, 1979 (Vol. 442) of the *Annals of the American Academy of Political and Social Science*, a useful issue dedicated to "The Human Dimension of Foreign Policy: An American Perspective."

become relatively non-unique, especially in sponsoring foreign scholars coming to the U.S. And many Americans who go abroad in the program tend to be sent for rather narrow and technical purposes rather than for the kind of an international exposure that achieves some breadth as a learning experience. At the least, the new agency is faced with the need to redefine the purpose, review the fields of study and categories of people who will be selected, and look to a special role for a program which is now one element in an exceedingly broad range of international movement in academia. If it is to maintain its prestige as governmental initiative and leadership for the interchange of ideas and a kind of mutual understanding that makes an international difference, the stature of participants and the forums at which they gather will need to be kept at a peak-of-the-field level. It will need to devote a larger portion of its exchange facilities to mature scholars or leaders—the ones who rise above the now sizeable mass of scholars, whose thinking makes the critical difference in the development of ideas, and who will contribute most to mutual understanding in the public domain in their respective countries. The goal would be to increase the amount of high quality and thoughtful communication that takes place on mutually important issues.

In all its exchange activities, ICA will have to find ways to respond to the growing reality that mutual understanding more frequently will come to mean some form of enlarged *multinational* and even global perspective for those who participate, rather than simply bilateral understanding. Therefore, ICA will need to take the lead for devising multilateral approaches for reaching this level and context of exchange. It was apparent in the course of conducting the pilot studies that such activities as multiregional seminars—sponsored problem-centered gatherings of specialists from various nations and regions of the world—were well received. They expanded participants' international perspective and their inclination to share experiences with colleagues. Further, for Third World participants such an approach provided an atmosphere of exchange among peers and avoided the previously mentioned embarrassing sponsor–client, competent–less competent, or rich man–poor man situation that is often part of a bilateral program in which foreign participants are invited individually. Such seminars also have the advantage of placing the U.S. in the role of a leader in the world forum of ideas, rather than that of propagandist. It is probable that the selection of topics for multinational seminars and similar programs will be one of ICA's most significant and far-reaching contributions.

Another facet of the official mutual understanding effort that has received extensive public attention is the attempt to explain America through its artistic and humanities accomplishment—Culture with a capital C. Art is seen as a significant medium for communicating the philosophical, intellectual, moral, and esthetic values and qualities of a people and their civilization. Exchange in this field has been promoted as a vital aspect of achieving mutual understanding, and other countries have taken a similar view. Along with literature, architecture, sculpture, painting, and so on, USIA and CU combined forces to present the performing arts. The range has been wide, from collegiate marching bands and choruses to symphony orchestras, from folk music and jazz to modern dance, from drama to ice shows, and from string quartets to rock groups. These tours have been highly visible and have attracted American domestic attention out of proportion to the relatively small part they play in the total program. Still, sometimes the effect in mutual understanding can be powerful. I had the good fortune to be in Venezuela when Leonard Bernstein and the New York Philharmonic came to perform. It was immediately after the downfall of the Perez Jimenez dictatorship in 1958, a particular triumph for the Venezuelan public that had forced an end to this dismal period in the country's history. The performance was held in the Aula Magna, a new architectural masterpiece on the National University campus that had never been used—the dictator did not permit gatherings. When that magnificent orchestra opened with the Venezuelan national anthem, a full house was on its feet, and there was not a dry eye Venezuelan or American!

Usually the event is less dramatic, to be sure, and sometimes a selection does not successfully cross the cultural or esthetic barrier at all. But cultural presentations do have a special role to play in official international communication relations. International sharing of creative and artistic achievement has merit *per se*. Everyone is the richer for it, and governments serve their constituents by facilitating such exchange. They do say something about a country that is not easily said otherwise, and they provide a special kind of communication link for important groups in modern societies that follow and appreciate the arts. In the Cold War and advocacy days, they were used to counterbalance the materialistic image to which America seemed to be vulnerable in the ideological competition of the time. But the genuine use of the arts as communication in content rather than image competition has been the main thrust.

Cultural presentations are also instruments of diplomacy with a kind of symbolic importance in nation-to-nation relations. They provide a nonpolitical and noncontroversial basis for governmental interaction when relations are otherwise strained, and enhance prospects for cooperation later in other areas. The fact that cultural exchange agreements were the first fruits of reopened relations with China is illustrative.

ICA will have to construct its rationale for future use of cultural presentations in an environment in which communication and media technology already permit unprecedented facilities for exchange in this field. The selection task is extraordinarily complicated. The American performing world is immense, the publishing world prolific, and artistic expression, both professional and amateur, has multiplied since these exchange activities were first initiated. Further, for artistic expression to reach its potential, there is a need to comprehend more clearly the cross-cultural aspect of artistic communication. For it must be recognized that while there is an elusive universal quality to artistic expression its transmission in accuracy and equivalence is far from guaranteed when it has to cross cultural gaps, especially if they are large ones, as, for example, between American and Indian art.

Finally, ICA still will have the front-line responsibility of determining just what is to be explained and said about the United States, whether for image purposes—which should be behind us—or for more accurate understanding. This is where professionalism as cross-national and cross-cultural communicators will be most in demand, and where analysis and research will need to be most astute to determine not just what Americans think should be stressed on the basis of their view of themselves but what other peoples need to have elucidated for their more dependable understanding. This is a direction of inquiry beyond the scope of this overview, but a few considerations for a new stance in presenting American society abroad will be considered in the next chapter.

8

FOR AMERICANS:
A NEW PERSPECTIVE,
A NEW STYLE,
A NEW DEFINITION OF INTERESTS

Presumably, the merit of trying to sort out the trends and changing factors that bear on international communication relationships is in providing a basis for projecting a future scenario and setting an agenda of adjustments and accommodations which will have to be made to adapt to changing times. Obviously there is some danger in attempting to address a very complex universe of communication matters with too limited a base for observation and analysis. Still, it is useful in a last chapter to talk in terms of agenda, and to note where the elements we have considered seem to lead as we look into the 1980s.

It is clear enough that very substantial changes have been taking place. When considered together, they add up to a profoundly altered milieu for carrying out all the extremely broad range of communication activities in which the United States and Americans are involved. Along with a radically new technological environment, the messages themselves flow in a greatly changed psychological climate compared with only two decades ago. The difficulty is that governments, organizations, and their managers tend not to be very adept at recognizing changes that challenge the logic of their institutionalized activity. And changing *communication* factors pose even more difficulty because communication itself is rarely considered to be the business at hand, but rather an adjunct aspect that is taken for granted. Relatively little studied attention is paid to it to know how it works, when it is not working as well as imagined, or when the fundamentals have changed. The thesis in this discussion is that the international communication process will have to receive more care and attention if it is to serve the needs of what we have called a *de facto* global society.

In effect, the question is whether the international communication process is to be an asset in coping with all the unprecedented demands for problem-solving that will go with an ever more interconnected world, or whether in its proneness to break down, it will be a liability. Can it be a more certain and reliable process by being better understood, or will the process be left by default to develop in its own spontaneous and artless way?

If there is any way to characterize succinctly the changing communication order as it affects the American position, it might be to suggest that one is asked to change the picture one holds of the way that the players in the international system interact. If it can be assumed that there is a global society dimension in the way that communication flows, then the old billiard ball conception of international relationships, in which nations act as discrete units, has to be abandoned. The reality in communication relationships is that there is no clicking of ricocheting balls. Rather, the subelements that make up the balls are interacting with those of other balls. For some purposes, the surfaces of the balls have lost much of their definition, and the "game" becomes very hard to follow. A nation will rarely speak with one voice. A systems-within-systems point of view has utility. It suggests that the United States and Americans as a society, for all the strength of their communication position, will be able to be effective and pursue increasingly complex interests only to the degree that they achieve the capacity to manage their communication affairs on many levels, and throughout an extensive and interrelated international system that pragmatically can be considered global.

For Americans, choosing how best to communicate in a global community is a more pressing matter than for others, for the United States is the biggest and most influential communicator and at the same time a nation very vulnerable to the success or failure of communication in world affairs. In some circles it has been suggested that the United States will fare better in these circumstances by assuming a more "mature" communication relationship with the rest of the world. This implies that by now Americans should have become more seasoned as a nation and more established in position, and that therefore the exaggerated self-importance and sensitivity to image and favorable attention characteristic of national adolescence should be left behind. Just what this more mature stance would consist of is never very well defined. But at least the implication is a more measured and sober, less emotional and evangelistic approach to its communication behavior. It implies a change in style, a decent respect for the interests and opinions of the rest of the world, a tolerance for difference, more of a negotiating and less of a chauvinistic stance. It does *not* imply actually being less powerful or influential.

That leaves the situation still rather vague, but Americans can be quite sure that their greater competence, leadership, and effectiveness as international communicators will contribute to their security and well-being in a demanding crowded world—and to that of the rest of the world as well. Big issues, such as arms control, defensive alliances, economic cooperation, and fair use of world resources, ultimately depend on it. So will many smaller matters. It is by the many facets of an effective communication process that knowledge regarding issues is shared, a sense of such common interests and purposes as exist can be sustained, and fear of the unknown can give way to confidence as greater understanding makes the other side's behavior more predictable. Negotiators can come more quickly to the merits of issues and positions. Or the reverse can be the result if the messages in effect are garbled, with the impact made worse by the speed and reach of modern technology. The point is that the communication statesmanship factor deserves to be taken much more specifically into account than it routinely is; for how the United States survives in the late twentieth century and beyond is going to depend on it as well as on other more recognized items such as power, political attractiveness, technical inventiveness, and cohesion as a nation.

Inevitably this summary agenda will be very open-ended, but it will be a way of going from the analysis to implications for what can be done. Let us note, then, a half dozen areas that invite purposeful thinking and planning if Americans are to turn in an effective performance in carrying out their international communication responsibilities.

SOME PROBLEM AREAS— AN AGENDA FOR AMERICANS

1. Increasing across-the-board Competence. In many ways Americans are relatively well-prepared for adapting to the realities of a fast changing and more interconnected world. They are used to change, even value it. They are pragmatic, accustomed to defining situations as problems to be solved. They are already a pluralistic society.

But Americans have distinct liabilities. They are not used to being dependent on outside man-made forces that they cannot control—and this will be the case in increasing interdependence. They are highly ethnocentric and more used to having the world interested in them and trying to understand them than in having it the other way around. Unlike Europeans, learning a foreign language and accepting the culture that goes with it is not their forte. And at the bottom of it all, they are not well-informed about the world outside their borders, either as a public or as elites that will have to be involved in it.

American international education may be going downhill. Indicators collected by the American Council on Education, for example, show that less than 2% of the high school graduates have any foreign language competence, and college enrollments in language courses have dropped some 30% in the 1970s. Less than 5% of teachers in training in 1973 received any exposure at all to international, comparative, area, or intercultural courses. While American 14-year-olds rank high in knowledge of their own state, local, and national affairs, they are far down the line in knowledge of world affairs compared with Europeans in the same age group. Less than 1% of America's college age group are enrolled in any courses covering international issues or areas. Less than 3% of those that are trained in the international field are employed in business, despite business's role in the international scene. The amount of media time and space that covers international items is small, and apparently more will not sell to the consumers. Fewer American correspondents now reside abroad than at any time since the end of World War II (Hayden, 1977).

In short, too few Americans receive from their exposure and education a mastery of the fundamentals required for an adequate international perspective.

As the United States is a country extraordinarily dedicated to specialized education and training of all kinds, including adult and in-service training, could not this shortcoming be remedied most efficiently by providing training specifically for those who find themselves working with international matters? The answer, of course, is no. In the first place, everyone needs much more civic literacy in world affairs just to be an effective citizen and make intelligent judgments. Secondly, waiting for the in-service occasion is too late. By that time resistance to attending to one's general competence is great. Taking a technical course, such as one in language, is acceptable; this meets a need for a supporting skill that one would not be expected to bring into the job. But going back to more general basics is threatening in the American professional culture. It simply seems too remedial for professional dignity. Businesses do very little in the international education of their employees who assume overseas responsibilities. Even the State Department's Foreign Service Institute, the facility specifically established to provide backstop training for government personnel engaged in foreign affairs, chronically stands at the end of the Department's line when budgets and assignments for training are made.

It is also difficult to draw a line between those who should be expected to have a substantial competence in the international dimension and those who will not need it. For example, as mentioned earlier, while success in the American political process requires first of all competence in *domestic* affairs, those who rise in it quickly become among the most important actors in the chain of influences by which *foreign* affairs decisions, large and small, are made. This includes elected officials, those who report and analyze political events, campaign managers, and the people who work with the voting public. But there is very little in the learning process through which Americans become successful politicians that prepares them to deal with international affairs. The civil service is another critical area. Relatively few positions specifically require an international education or foreign experience. Yet civil service decisions have impact on a vast and vital array of government activity with international significance. The taxpayers would howl, or course, but it is tempting to recommend a large allocation of Fulbright grants for key civil servants to study abroad. The investment would pay off handsomely.

Actually, the root problem is in breaking out of the intellectual processes that come with ethnocentricity so that beyond just building up factual information, one would become oriented to cultural difference itself and to the implications for international communication. Even if one's communication is with foreign people whose own international experience with Americans reduces most of the barrier, it is nevertheless useful to be able to place one's counterparts in their own communication setting in their own society in order to appreciate how much of a split personality they must have to enter into cosmopolitan international interchange. Americans have less occasion to be bicultural persons themselves because today's cosmopolitan internationalized culture is so heavily influenced by American culture to begin with.

The fact that English is being used so much more extensively and serves American travel needs and even routine business needs would seem to reduce the pressure to learn foreign languages. If the language learning intention is not more than looking toward a mechanical means of getting along, the need probably is reduced. But to be more responsive to the problem, two points need to be made. One is that the skill objective should be enlarged—rather than learning how to say it in French, the goal should be to learn to communicate with French people. This leaves language *per se* only part of the learning process. Language should be more than simply the means for finding the train station. It should be an entree into the thought processes of the people with whom one would communicate.

Second, the time has come for a new sense of proportion as to what is needed for international communication. Language as part of communication skill is important, but still more important is the ability to factor cultural difference into the communication task at hand, to appreciate the culture concept itself. It is a matter of seeing culture as psychological behavior that is at the heart of communication processes, and the ability to recognize one's own ethnocentricity and know what part of American behavior is a product of American culture and not a universal aspect of human nature. Intercultural communication should be the main subject—to which language learning is added as necessary, rather than the reverse as is now the case—if the broader aspects of communicating across the barriers of culture and national experience are to be considered at all.

Only a start has been made in this direction in the United States. Fortunately, recognition of multiculturalism in America, even if it poses a dilemma where melting pot values are traditional, does give occasion for bending educational philosophy toward recognizing the part that cultural difference plays. To the extent that this insight is turned toward international communication as well, an addition will be made in American competence for coping with a multicultural world society.

2. Communicating from a Position of Predominant Bigness and Power. In the future, the United States will need to reflect the kind of communication statesmanship that goes with the self-assurance of being a senior partner in the world communication process. Being the biggest is the hardest part to play, and much depends on the style with which it is exercised.

Americans take great satisfaction in their achievements and technological prowess, and in their standard of living that both rewards and symbolizes achievement. Unhappily this too often results in what is seen as a patronizing, almost boastful outward behavior that impedes communication. To other national groups, especially to developing nations, it more frequently is disturbing that the U.S. uses up such a large share of world resources, and seems to do so at their expense. When the Americans also reflect a sense of moral superiority in their accomplishment, imply a lack of the same where achievement is not up to their standard, and then further use their accomplishment as license to be prescriptive, then bigness and power become a liability.

Unfortunately, this condescending air can be perceived— particularly if a critic works at it—in many situations in which Americans feel their motives are benevolent. It also can be perceived from abroad when our discussions are not intended for an overseas audience. Congressional debate, for example, is transmitted overseas as fast as to the Congressman's local district. The debate on the Panama Canal treaty might be reviewed with this in mind. Congressional intention in decreeing that foreign assistance "reach the poorest of the poor," or our sponsorship of the Peace Corps, might signal a bit of it. Mexico's long stand-offishness from American AID might be a reaction to such a perception.

Thus, bigness works to complicate what is being heard by both sides. Being big with no pretense at dignity makes it worse, of course, as in telling the world that the United States will not be kicked around by little powers like Panama or Cambodia (in the Mayaguez incident). But pretending not to be big is not very convincing either. False and transparent modesty, the unnecessary rush to self-criticism, too much deference to insignificant actors on the world's stage on the presumption that they too are "equal" sovereign states may at best make Americans feel that they have been fully democratic.

Whatever statesmanship in bigness will consist of, being ready and able to hear what the other party is trying to say and to seek the meaning of it must be part of it. Certainly if Americans are to build up an empathy with the rest of the world, a place to start would be an attempt to capture the sense of what it is like to be on the receiving end of American dominance, whether it is a matter of receiving disaster relief, technical assistance, military advice, or just having to feel the repercussions and effects of what the United States does in the international arena in general. American government decisions and many others as well can be as important abroad as at home. Yet this is too rarely taken into account in American interaction with the rest of the world, even when Americans have to puzzle over the very reactions generated by the psychological discomfort of always being on the receiving end.

Actually, in historical perspective and in comparison with other world powers, the United States has exercised a considerable sense of responsibility in wielding its power and resources. This is generally recognized by neutral observers. But the self-righteousness with which Americans have carried out their international activities has sometimes adversely affected communication relationships. When there has been suspicion of American motives, this stance has become more unbearable. In any case, the line between actions that are taken in American self-interest and those taken in the interest of international community is a fine one. Often the interest is mutual, but not always as mutual as Americans think. It is how a given action is perceived that counts in the communication process, and a mismatch in perception is probably more frequent than realized. Some analysts note that the U.S. sometimes makes its attempt to rationalize its motives more of a problem than necessary. They suggest that people in other nations assume that the United States will take some advantage of its position as a matter of course, and that this is understandable. What is confusing is excessive zeal in honoring commitments beyond reason (e.g., in Viet Nam) or in overstating a selfless motive. They think we do protest too much, and this undermines confidence. Just how the U.S. gains and loses "credibility" is a remarkably unstudied matter.

By any serious projection, the world community will need some extraordinarily astute leadership. This role logically goes to the large nations, and especially to the one with the largest communication resources. This is to be expected. Reticence will not be helpful nor will it be expected; not using a strong position would be censured by those who must depend on big-power leadership. The task is to learn how to do it, to learn how to be the most powerful communicator the world has ever known.

3. Ideological Considerations for the Future.

In all the reference made in this study to a changing world environment—new lifestyles, new governments, new international arrangements, and all the rest—the most fundamental change inevitably will be found in what happens to ideas and guiding principles. In a climate in which almost everyone is exploring to a greater or lesser degree, the task for Americans is to take a new grip on their role as innovators and champions of ideology and ideas, the role that both has made the U.S. one of the world's special resources for such, and has given it a special kind of security in alliances and cooperation.

The task will be one of reviewing the values that the U.S. has projected internationally for consistency with international concerns, of recognizing where these concerns might have changed in the United States itself, and distinguishing which are fundamental and which fall more into the category of emotional associations with cherished ways of doing things. (Americans place great importance on the voting process, for example, but the underlying value is in making government responsive to the will of the people.) Which values bear no compromise abroad, and which are possibly more relevant to American society than to others? How far will the United States go in its advocacy? In its insistence and even policing? To what extent is an American conception of values universal, and to what culturally or situationally relative?

All this is painful business, but it must be the subject of hard analysis in today's international communication relationships. There is much more suspicion of universal values today. There are more questions as to how they apply, in what priority, and especially whether one country has a monopoly on them. If American values are to help set the pattern that will come to characterize a more global society, Americans will have to be very astute in recognizing wherein their ideological patterns apply at home because they have become uniquely institutionalized in the special conditions of American life, and wherein they can be broadly applied. Most difficult of all will be recognizing where ideological functional prerequisites differ with culture and circumstance. The point is that American leadership will be needed, badly needed in the fermenting international community, and also that America itself needs to assure its continuing role. If America is not a source of moral leadership, its position will erode to being but one power (albeit a large one), negotiating in the marketplace simply of trading off power and resources. This problem area is one of the most difficult, for it is the one in which issues are seen from such differing perspectives both overseas and at home, the one in which emotion and ethnocentricism can lead to such uncompromising dogmatism and even religious zeal that rational review and discussion are greatly impeded.

We know that the *political* ideological front has become much less polarized internationally, more fragmented among the initiatives and perceived special priorities of leaders in their separate countries. Ideology as such has become less the dominant subject of international communication, at least in the sense of the central "isms." We know that the American model is seen less monolithically, as is that of the Soviet Union; few nations see them as completely importable systems. In developing countries and in changing modern countries as well there will be variations of these model themes, mutations, partial borrowings, and entirely different creations. Already the United States has seen a sharp decline in detailed interest in its institutions in favor of experimentation by leaders in other countries with patterns that will be either more expedient or more congenial to a local sense of cultural consistency.

We also know that *economic* subjects have become as important, or even more important, than political concerns in ideological debate. Accordingly, the value issues shift to economic affairs—what is the social purpose to be served in production and distribution of goods? What is the proper role of government in the economy? Should unlimited growth yield to other objectives?

After a rather low ideological profile during U.S. extrication from Viet Nam, Watergate, and through some years of introspection regarding value orientations within American society, the country has reached out internationally again with its renewed emphasis on human rights. It immediately became clear that this thrust was going to require more fine-tuning than was anticipated by the Carter administration in its haste to again project an American moral position both as a basis for world leadership and to renew a sense of purpose at home. All the difficulties in ideological advocacy came to the surface: Where does ideological enthusiasm leave off and international political expedience begin? By what virtue does the U.S. presume to advocate—how is its own performance on human rights actually perceived abroad? Whether right or wrong, is the American prescriptive role as acceptable as before? And in any case, by what philosophical orientation or system of cultural values is one to define precisely what human rights are?

There is some new analysis going on today to explore the degree to which human rights is a culturally relative subject as differing combinations of underlying values define rights in differing social systems. Muslim society, for example, inevitably starts with a drastically different definition, for the value system goes back to the social thinking embodied in the Koran. Simply getting the American view of human rights adopted in a U.N. resolution does not go very far in such cases. One of the more general contrasts in orientation that affects the human rights debate is to be found in the distinction made between placing priority value on the individual, or on the group. Most traditional societies, some modern ones, and all of the ones having to resolve the problems generated by very dense populations tend at least to assume that *groups* have *some* rights too. The American attention has been on the individual, of course, and American definitions of rights follow from that. Americans also see political rights as primary; others place more importance on economic or other kinds of rights. Even in the United States there is now more concern with economic rights than in an earlier era.

There possibly has been more international discussion of a greater variety of ideological matters than Americans realize, for much of it has taken place outside the U.S.-versus-U.S.S.R. context, and during the time that Americans have been preoccupied with moral issues within the United States. If American thinking on ideology and moral purpose is to contribute a basis for solving the problems that go with a new pluralistic phase of international relationships, both communication style and value content will need to be carefully considered for actual effect and consequences.

4. Getting and Interpreting the International News. Because Americans operate as an information society, above all others they will have a reason to pursue the question: how can people be assured that they get optimum quality and reliable interpretation in their international news? In effect, the future basic question for Americans and for others as well is: how good is the international central nervous system? For in coping today, information, messages, and signals are basic. Therefore, it is hard to overestimate the importance of accuracy, selection, and interpretation in the international news as it flows through news channels from reporters and editors to public use. As news and media institutions and technology intensify their dominance over public information, these channels will be the overwhelming determinant as to what is defined as news, how it is conceptualized, which issues get attention and which not.

This will not be simply a problem for the news institutions and the government. The public role is not passive, and its greater awareness of what news it needs and of what quality, and its insistence on getting it, will have much to do with how well it is internationally educated.

All this places a heavy responsibility on the American press and on journalism, print and electronic. The journalists' calling becomes still higher as its function expands from being the fourth estate within the society to primary gatekeeper between the American public and the world of events taking place beyond American borders. As their mission becomes more international, journalists are asked to transmit both news and its meaning. Given the present organization of international news services, they will have this mission for outgoing news as well. Having to communicate the context of the news as well as the facts is what makes this a different kind of professionalism as compared with domestic journalism where more of a consumer ability to grasp the meaning of events can be assumed.

It then becomes a part of the public interest to question the preparation that goes into the journalist profession. There is no bar examination or medical board to pass. It follows that the international dimension to a journalist's education becomes far more important than that of the general public, or even that of many other elites who work in international affairs. For the news profession is, in the final analysis, the data source for Americans, the programmer for their computers. And the rule applies here as in all computer programming—garbage in, garbage out. As television transmits larger portions of the news, the worry is that it is too often packaged to attract an audience; newscasters are judged by how well they come across. The challenge posed for both the public and the media is to find a way to look beyond these superficialities and make the system produce an optimum-quality service in supplying the public data base. Being maturely informed is part of achieving that elusive "mature" communication relationship with the rest of the world. One implication may be that the day of the all-purpose foreign correspondent should be over. The quick visit to cover a breaking event, or accompanying high officials on their whirlwind overseas trips, makes for risky reporting. Few professionals have that broad a command of the world beat. It takes the most carefully prepared people backed by the best news agencies to do an adequate job. At the least, more area-specialized reporters, and the training which goes with that specialization, will be needed.

Given their position and responsibility, Americans have perhaps the greatest need of all people of the world to attend to their requirement for quality news. But the need is virtually worldwide, with greater or smaller portions of national publics seriously involved. Therefore, it is clearly in the American national interest to encourage and support increasing professionalism and international competence in foreign news networks also. Our global society's central nervous system will have to be as reliable as possible.

5. Research and Development for International Communication. Americans have made spectacular research and development progress in a long list of specialized fields from medicine to astrophysics, but not in international communication. In this field we know very little, even at a fundamental level. There is a certain amount of descriptive research and data available, to be sure. The volume of communication traffic can be estimated, at least via certain channels; the export of books and magazines can be tallied; the market for news service is regularly surveyed. Public opinion polls can give some idea of contrasting views of international issues. But even this kind of information is not systematically gathered. When charges are made regarding Western domination of news flow to the Third World, both the charges and the rebuttals depend more on rhetoric than on hard statistics. Generally, no one has wanted to know the facts badly enough to go to the effort to research them. UNESCO collects statistics, but these come from government sources and vary widely in accuracy—and, of course, as official figures they cannot be challenged.

We know even less that is scientifically respectable about the dynamics of the international communication process itself. What makes an event "news" in different places? What makes people believe a report as against enjoying it as entertainment? How do gatekeepers work in varying societies? What are the cross-cultural factors that determine how people perceive information and reason about it? How do images of other nations form, how persistent are they, what makes them change? After a spate of interest in these subjects in the 1950s and early 1960s, they have received relatively little research attention, at least as applied to the international field.

There has been almost no research done that systematically establishes just what it is in cultural differences that leads to misperceptions and miscommunication between specific national groups—between Brazilians and Americans, or Egyptians and Americans, for example. Fortunately, some substantial and excellent work has been done on American–Japanese communication, with social scientists on both sides cooperating in the effort. Some research has been directed at communication between businessmen and among corporation directors. Looking at the way decision making is understood and perceived in the two societies has facilitated cooperation among managers. There are bits and pieces of research available for other sets of national relationships too, but often these add up to little more than general hints for the traveller, or guides to help Americans make initial sense of "foreign" behavior. Some of this helps us understand the noise factor discussed in Chapter 6. For many countries there is a certain amount of ethnographic material available, but it is not organized for application to the problems of those who would communicate. Many problems could be eased by knowing more specifically just what aspects of American behavior pose difficulties—for Kenyans, for instance, and vice versa—and why when seen in the context of unique experience and culture factors on each side.

Despite its importance in international negotiation, very little inquiry has been directed at differing styles of reasoning, styles of debate, use of evidence, or patterns of reacting to new information. Such inquiry as has been attempted has only reached the preliminary and exploratory stages of research. In the early post-World War II period philosophers began some inquiry into this dimension—F. S. C. Northrup's *Meeting of East and West* (1946) comes to mind—as did linguistic anthropologists. But much of this work was abandoned in the trend toward research subjects that lent themselves more to empirical methods and to more limited-range theory building.

In short, there is a research and development task posed now of very substantial proportions. It is not a matter of a few foundation grants for a few team research projects. It will require an effort more on the order of the national attempt to understand cancer, or at least that of the Defense Education Act in its support for Area Studies or a Ford/Rockefeller search for new methods in tropical agriculture. The effort will have to be multidisciplinary and multinational; it will require the collaboration of the practitioners. It would take an initial project just to establish research priorities and a framework for coordinating a larger program. But the possibilities are intriguing for it is a very open field, and good research could be of such far-reaching utility.

6. Legitimizing a New Subject in International Relations. If the international communication dimension is as important an aspect of international relations as we have argued here, it might well be the subject of a "great issue" debate. At a minimum it merits a proper place in the attention of the foreign affairs community, and needs to be legitimized as an integral concern of international relations analysis, just as foreign commerce, economic development, conflict resolution, or the role of international organizations have become standard components of the foreign affairs field. Communication simply needs more stature than it now has in the foreign affairs inquiry. It does not seem to have the immediacy as an issue or the glamour of impending armed conflict to attract heated discussion and debate. But there is every reason to consider it one of the basic subjects for various levels of international relations attention, from university departments to diplomatic circles.

The point is that it will be difficult to take concerted action to rationally conduct the international communication relations of the United States until it becomes part of the normal and even institutionalized concerns of the foreign affairs establishment. It is only when recognized foreign affairs specialists make speeches on the subject, congressional committees hold hearings, pundits write about it on the editorial pages, and illustrous leaders talk about the coming crisis in communication in graduation speeches that a critical mass of minds will be engaged. This progression has only begun. The problem posed for Americans is to find a way to prompt its intellectual leadership to articulate the basic issues of American communication with the rest of the world, to stimulate debate, and make the subject part of the public domain to be considered along with other national concerns.

Beyond the present foreign affairs leadership, another target stands out for stimulating greater attention to the communication dimension. This is the academic community, especially the departments that perform in teaching and research in international relations and train professionals at the graduate level. Here is where the array of subjects that supposedly apply to understanding foreign affairs have become crusty with institutionalization and where updating is in order. Much current training for the international relations field reflects the reality of several decades ago, rather than the needs of today. A student would probably get more use now from a course in the role of the press in foreign affairs than from International Law, and he would more likely have occasion to use it. More answers in understanding how the international relations process works might be found in studying how nations communicate, and miscommunicate, than in pursuing macro models that, for example, correlate aggression with GNP, or with any of the other characteristics of a nation that are scanned by computer-assisted international behavior research projects.

A start has been made. For graduate level and research emphasis, the Massachusetts Institute of Technology has been a pioneer in studying communication aspects of international affairs. The Fletcher School of Law and Diplomacy, whose graduates are to be found in an extraordinary range of key foreign affairs positions—from American ambassadorships to international organizations—has had its Edward R. Murrow Center for Public Diplomacy in operation for more than a decade. At the undergraduate level, Georgetown University's School of Foreign Service, the nation's oldest and largest school in this specialty, also has been placing increasing emphasis on the communication dimension. The International Studies Association now schedules more sessions of its annual conference for communication-related topics, reflecting increased interest and activity on the part of its professional membership.

CONCLUDING NOTE

"Global society," then, is a concept neither too fuzzy nor too abstract to be realistic. It is not something to be for or against, or to dismiss as the turf of the idealistic or dreamy one-world enthusiasts. It is a reality that faces leaders of most nations, and most especially those of the United States who confront a heavy task in seeing clearly what is happening in world sociology, what the salient trends are, and what problems have to be met.

It is certain that the "infrastructure" required for meeting global dimension problems—to borrow a developer's term—will have to include a highly effective practice in international communication. For all its importance, it is disquieting to consider the extent to which this capability has been left to develop by force of circumstance and spontaneous factors, to realize how relatively unstudied and unanalyzed it is. With an explosion in communication technology, the implications posed by more intensive communicating around the world have multiplied while minds are just now being engaged in assessing the meaning and outcome. There is some urgency in asking the right questions *now*.

The essential inquiry requires projection into the future. This poses an extraordinarily difficult task, for this is a matter not only of extrapolating from present trends and emerging new factors to their probable development through the 1980s and 1990s, but of projecting them in their *combination* and within an evolving world society that is becoming more global in many other ways as well.

The complexity of the American task in navigating this changing stream can be appreciated, if only in broad outline, by simply singling out certain of the major items treated in this discussion, and anticipating how they together will set a demanding coping task.

—The momentum of communicating technological ingenuity will seek its application even before public needs for it are felt. It will produce a drum beat of impacts on lifestyles and on social and political institutions.

—The gap between the First and Third Worlds in communication capability and advantage most probably will grow. This will generate more insistent demands for international arrangements for its management and access.

—The U.S. appetite and that of other advanced information societies for gathering and consuming news and information can be expected to grow, with the need increasing for reliable *international* news and information as the net of interdependent relationships draws tighter.

—The American threat to the national sovereignty and national advantage of other nations will be felt more intensely as nations try to stay abreast of communication developments affecting their vital interests. Related issues will become more political and less technical in treatment.

—Foreign affairs policy-making will have an ever-increasing public dimension to take into account, and the opinions and perceptions of issues held by both domestic and foreign publics will be standard considerations. One possible liability in this is that the U.S. visibility, already disproportionately high, will become further accentuated because of its position in communication flow.

—Despite diffusion of an America-centered internationalized culture, global scale communication will more directly inject long-standing cultural differences and contrasting philosophical assumptions into international affairs. This in turn will make it harder for Americans to understand world social and political forces that affect them and their international activities.

—While English will dominate modern international communication to an American advantage, its utility will be deceptive as many highly significant nuances of meaning, styles of reasoning, implicit philosophy, moral fundamentals, emotional motivation, and ethnocentric outlooks will fail to be transmitted. English-speaking people will be led to assume that they have a greater degree of understanding than will be the case.

—Entertainment via new communication technology—including a higher visual content—will press ever harder against restraints to the flow of popular culture. The social and cultural impact of the U.S. abroad will be of greater concern almost everywhere, with Third World societies especially affected.

—An increasing number of Americans interacting internationally through transnational organizations and enterprises, as well as in official international agencies, will expand the base of Americans conducting some form of U.S. international relations. Their competence will be ever more essential in the national interest.

—Communication resources will be still more vital in commercial, economic, and security fields, and the U.S. will find that this component more often will be the subject of hard bargaining.

—American resources in higher education, especially in modern technical application, will continue to be in high demand, at least until regional capabilities fill the present gap.

More could be recapped here, and the trends could be stated in varying ways. However, the point is that, unlike population or world resources, no major attempt has been made to project communication potentialities into the future to try to anticipate the implications either for global society or for individual nations. We may find that the drama of science fiction will apply more than we are prepared to accept as trends are extended into the 21st century. It takes no fantasy, however, or Club of Rome-sized inquiry to appreciate the central role that communication will play in human affairs in the rest of this century—or the worldwide reverberations that will be felt as the United States exercises its central communication position, whether by design or simply in the course of conducting its normal but far-reaching business.

BIBLIOGRAPHY

Academy for Educational Development. *The United States and the debate on the world information order*. Washington, D.C.: Academy for Educational Development, 1978.

Aggarwala, N. Press freedom: A third world view. *Exchange*, 178, *Winter*, 18–20.

Almond, G. A. & Verba, S. *The civic culture: Political attitudes and democracy in five nations*. Boston: Little, Brown, 1963.

Asia Society. *Asia in American textbooks*. New York: Asia Society, 1976.

Aspen Institute for Humanistic Studies. Coping with Interdependence, 1975.

Ball, G. W. *Diplomacy for a crowded world*. Boston: Little, Brown, 1976.

Center for Strategic and International Studies. *International information, education, and cultural relations: Recommendations for the future*. Washington, D.C.: Center for Strategic and International Studies, Special Report Number Fifteen, 1975.

Coleman, R. & Rainwater, L. *Social standing in America: New dimensions of class*. New York: Basic Books, 1978.

d'Arcy, J. Direct broadcast satellites and the right to communicate. *EBU Review*, 1969, *118*, 14–18.

Dillon, W. S. *Gifts and nations: The obligation to give, receive, and repay*. The Hague and Paris: Mouton, 1968.

Fisher, G. *Public diplomacy and the behavioral sciences*. Bloomington: Indiana University Press, 1972.

Gergen, K. & Gergen, M. What other nations hear when the eagle screams. *Psychology Today,* June 1974, 53.

Gunter, J. F. An introduction to the great debate. *Journal of Communication,* 1978, *Autumn,* 142–156.

Hall. E. T. *The silent language*. Garden City, N.Y.: Doubleday, 1959.

Halle, L. J. *The cold war as history*. New York: Harper & Row, 1967.

Harms, L. S. & Richstad, J. (Eds.) *Evolving perspectives on the right to communicate*. Honolulu, HI: East–West Center, East–West Communication Institute, 1977.

Harms, L. S., Richstad, J., & Kie, K. A. (Eds.) *Right to communicate: Collected papers.* Honolulu, HI: University of Hawaii Press, 1977.

Hayden, R. L. Global education for the 21st century. *International Studies Notes of the International Studies Association, 1977, Fall,* 19–23.

Hoopes, T. *The devil and John Foster Dulles.* London: Andre Deutsch, 1974.

Horton, P. (Ed.) *The third world and press freedom.* New York: Praeger, 1978.

Imai, M. *Never take yes for an answer.* Tokyo: Simul Press, 1975.

Isaacs, H. *Scratches on our minds.* New York: John Day, 1958.

Janis, I. L. *Victims of groupthink.* New York: Houghton Mifflin, 1972.

Jervis, R. *Perception and misperception in international politics.* Princeton, N.J.: Princeton University Press, 1976.

Kaunda, K.D. *Humanism in Zambia and a guide to its implementation,* Part I. Lusaka, Zambia: Government Printer. (See also Part II.)

Kellermann, H. J. *Cultural relations as an instrument of U.S. foreign policy—The educational exchange program between the United States and Germany 1945–1954.* Washington, D.C.: Department of State Publication #8931, 1978.

Kendrick, A. *Prime time: The life of Edward R. Murrow.* Boston: Little, Brown, 1967.

Kraar, L. Singapore—The country run like a corporation. *Fortune Magazine,* July 1974, 85–89, 152–154.

Lefever, E. W. (Ed.) *Morality and foreign policy: A symposium on President Carter's stance.* Washington, D.C.: Georgetown University Ethics and Public Policy Center, Monograph Series, 1977.

Leidel, D. *Black to black images—America and Africa.* Unpublished papers, Department of State Senior Seminar in Foreign Policy, 1973.

Lewis, M. The blind spot of U.S. foreign intelligence. *Journal of Communication,* 1976, *Winter,* 44–55.

Luard, E. *Types of international society.* New York: Macmillan, 1976.

Nordenstreng, K. & Schiller, H. I. (Eds.) *National sovereignty and international communication.* Norwood, N.J.: Ablex Publishing Corporation, 1979.

Northrop, F. S. C. *The meeting of east and west.* New York: Macmillan, 1946.

Overseas Liaison Committee *An analysis of U.S.–Iranian cooperation in higher education.* Washington, D.C.: American Council on Education, 1976.

Read, W. H. *America's mass media merchants.* Baltimore, MD.: Johns Hopkins University Press, 1976.

Richardson, J., Jr. Mutual understanding revisited. *Exchange,* 1975, *Summer,* 6–10.

Richardson, J., Jr. (Spec. Ed.) The human dimension of foreign policy: An American perspective. *Annals of the American Academy of Political and Social Science,* March, 1979, Vol. 442.

Rosenblum, M. Reporting from the third world. *Foreign Affairs,* 1977, *55,* **4,** 815–835.

Stoessinger, J. *Nations in darkness: China, Russia, and America.* New York: Random House, 1971.

Tunstall, J. *The media are American.* New York: Columbia University Press, 1977.

UNESCO Statistical Yearbook, 1976.

United States Department of State, Bureau of Educational and Cultural Affairs. *Communicating for Understanding.* Washington, D.C.: U.S. Government Printing Office, 1976.

Useem, J., Useem, R., & Donoghue, J. Men in the middle of the third culture: The roles of American and nonwestern people in cross–cultural administration. *Human Organization,* 1963, *22,* 169–179.

AUTHOR INDEX

Page numbers in *italics* indicate where complete references are listed.

SUBJECT INDEX

State Department; Foreign Service, 43-44,
 129
Students, foreign in U.S., 19, 22, 99-103

T

Television, impact of, 4, 58, 72-75
Transnational organizations, 7, 17, 97, 125,
 156

U

United Nations, 15, 27, 28, 59, 75
UNESCO, 57, 62-64, 70, 124, 152
United Press International, 61
United States Information Agency, 2, 9,
 33-34, 36, 39, 55, 114, 116, 118, 131-
 139

V

Venezuela, 23, 64, 99, 138
Viet Nam, 10, 16, 27, 28, 35, 52, 127, 129
Voice of America, 2, 9, 55, 62, 131, 134

W

World Administrative Radio Conference,
 58, 59
World Press Freedom Committee, 63

Y

Youth for Understanding, 19

Z

Zambia, 40, 41, 86, 95, 96